FAMILIES
of the
JAILED

MARGARET STEVENS
and
RODGER STEVENS

WALSCH
W
BOOKS

an imprint of
HAMPTON ROADS
PUBLISHING COMPANY, INC.
www.hrpub.com

Cover design by Marjoram Productions
Cover art by Index Stock and Picture Quest
Author photos © Kathy Hollis Cooper
Professional Photography

For information write:
Hampton Roads Publishing Company, Inc.
1125 Stoney Ridge Road
Charlottesville, VA 22902
804-296-2772
fax: 804-296-5096
e-mail: hrpc@hrpub.com
www.hrpub.com

If you are unable to order this book from your local
bookseller, you may order directly from the publisher.
Call 1-800-766-8009, toll-free.
Library of Congress Catalog Card Number: 00-111928

ISBN 1-57174-277-8

10 9 8 7 6 5 4 3 2 1

Printed on acid-free paper in Canada

To my children, Rodger, David, and Ann, and to my grandchildren, Morgan, Jason, Jed, and Erin, all of whom are the greatest blessings in my life.

To Grace Wittenberger, my spiritual mentor and close friend for nearly fifty years. Her continual calm, deep faith has inspired and sustained my family and me through many dark days and nights.

Finally, to the many members of our extended family, the countless friends in all parts of the world, who have believed in Rodger and prayed for his total freedom.

To one and all, thank you from the bottom of my heart, and God bless you!

Acknowledgments

My deepest appreciation to Neale Donald Walsch for his instant interest and constant support of this book. In a chance meeting in the Los Angeles airport, he offered to publish and distribute it, after drawing in my notebook a sketch of the book and its title, which was his inspiration.

Many thanks to Karen Williams for her sensitive and skillful editing of the first draft of a very rough manuscript.

Deep appreciation to Pat Florin for her skillful, sensitive editing and typing of the final manuscript.

My thanks and gratitude to Dr. Gerald Jampolsky for so graciously giving us permission to use portions of his wonderfully helpful book *Forgiveness*.

And to Dr. Catherine Ponder, a dear friend for more than thirty years, for her guidance, inspiration, and encouragement through her many books, and for her personal support through this difficult time in our lives.

Finally, to my family and many friends for their loyalty and steadfastness, for their encouragement and unconditional love throughout the eight years of this challenge.

Above all, my growing appreciation of Spirit for stretching and enlarging my understanding of its power, provision, and limitless love, expressed as motivation and support as I attempted to express what was deep in my heart.

Table of Contents

Foreword

This is a stunning book. Simply stunning.

It is stunning not only because it addresses something that is virtually ignored by our society—the shock, the anger, the pain, the confusion, the rejection, the turmoil, and the emotional, physical, and spiritual challenges faced by families of the jailed, and by the imprisoned themselves—but because of the way in which it addresses these things.

It is stunning because of its compassion and its vision, the sweep of its awareness and the sensitivity of its observations, the depth of its insights and the very real, very practical value of its suggestions.

It is stunning because it provides assistance, not merely commentary; solutions, not merely descriptions; tools for living, not merely topics for discussion.

It is stunning most of all because of the love and the healing that flows from its pages—at a time when love and healing are what is needed most.

The guilt or innocence of the person jailed is irrelevant. This book is not about guilt or innocence, right or wrong. It is about rising above whatever has happened, for whatever reason, and turning the unbearable into the bearable. It is about not only facing the problem, but becoming larger than the problem. It is about not only handling adversity, but overcoming it—and actually changing it into a gift.

That's right, I said a gift.

Hard as it is to believe, this book may be able to shift your point of view about what is occurring so dramatically that you will not only be able to "live with" what is happening, you will actually see the blessing in it, for you and for others, and at last rest more easily, knowing that something much larger is at work here than you might ever have imagined.

Each person walks his or her path, and we know not why those paths lead them to where they do. But we can know that there is perfection in the process, and when we come to understand that, we can also know peace. Yet here is a great secret: perfection is there when we place it there.

This book shows us how.

If you have a family member who is going to jail or is in jail, this book can change your life.

If you know of someone who has a family member going to jail or in jail, give them this book. It could be the greatest help you ever offered.

If you are in the helping profession and are working with others in these circumstances, recommend this book. It could provide some of the best advice you could possibly supply.

If you are in jail, please read this book. Its message could allow you to see that your life is far from over. That you have worth as a person. That there is much of value yet for you to give. And that, most of all, you need not be alone or lonely, frightened or angry, filled with despair or hopelessness, overcome by bitterness or frustration, but can yet fashion a life of contribution and of substance, of meaning and of purpose, whether you are Inside or Out.

For all who come to these pages, this book could turn your thoughts about life in jail inside out.

In this book are the voices of hope. They are the voices of Margaret Stevens, a woman in her eighties whose world was turned upside down by the sudden incarceration of her son, and of Rodger Stevens, the incarcerated.

They talk here not so much about how to survive "inside"—how to get cigarettes or books in, provide cash or other necessities, how to behave at visitations, or any of the usual things covered in some other pamphlets and books that have been developed around this topic. Instead, Margaret and Rodger talk about the more intangible aspects of this experience, the aspects that actually determine what the experience is going to be.

You may not be able to adopt all of the attitudes or accept all of the understandings or agree with all of the points of view that are expressed here. Yet if you will explore all of them, I feel sure you will find a resonance with some of them. And if that winds up being only one or two of them, you will still have found here something of enormous value.

Listen, then, to these voices of hope. They can heal a heart and a spirit that have been broken. They speak to you now at your request, for you have called for this help or you would not be holding this book in your hand.

This is how God works.

Believe it.

—Neale Donald Walsch
author, *Conversations with God*

Introduction

When our lives flow along in relative order and comfort, it is easy to become complacent. We read about tragedies happening to other people, feel a twinge of sympathy, then slip back into preoccupation with our own concerns. Perhaps a serious problem presents itself in the life of a friend or acquaintance and we get somewhat more involved.

And then, for many of us, *it* happens. Life hands us a *huge* challenge, and we find ourselves suddenly filled with confusion, fear, even hopelessness. Where do we turn? What do we do?

This simple book is written by two people whose lives were drastically changed by an unexpected imprisonment. Rodger, the prisoner, is of course most affected, but as his mother, I have also found this to be a life-changing situation. All our family members, in fact, are deeply affected and involved in trying to find answers. We would like to share this book with those who are going through similar challenges.

We, mother and son, have both found that our deepest, most troubling questions are answered in the framework of a strong faith in God. But we hope that the suggestions we present may be helpful to you and your family, regardless of your beliefs. Take what works for you.

The ideas and practices that we share have moved us from a place of despair, cynicism, and hopelessness to a new sense of acceptance, forgiveness, and trust in a power that is greater than any justice system devised by humankind. The end is still not in sight for us, but our faith is stronger than ever, and we know Who will have the final say in this drama. That word will be the perfect solution, with good to all concerned.

Our Story

"The world is round, and the place that seems like
the end may only be the beginning."

—Nineteenth-century author
Ella Wheeler Wilcox

I closed my eyes to shut out the bleak surroundings, but my mind could not block out the grief on the face of the elderly woman who sat beside me. She shifted her weight on the hard metal bench, her worn sweater scant protection against the chill of the waiting room. At her feet, two small boys played with bottle caps and a paper cup. I had the feeling that this was not a new experience for them. They played together wordlessly until the younger boy climbed up on the woman's lap and asked, "When can we see Daddy? Why won't they let us sit on his lap and hug him? Why, Grandma?" The tired woman sighed, shook her head, and held the child close, gently kissing the top of his head.

Across from me, a white-haired couple sat holding hands. The woman wept silently. The man handed her a tissue and patted her shoulder. She looked at him through red-rimmed eyes and said faintly, "I don't know how much longer I can do this, John. Six months we've been coming here for visits through thick glass, not able to touch him, careful what we say, afraid of talking about something that could get him into more trouble. . . ." Her voice trailed off. "What have we done to bring this suffering into our family? Where did we go wrong?"

I have spent thirty years working as a minister, and have been witness to suffering of all kinds, but never encountered an environment of such hopelessness as this waiting room. The very air seemed charged with grief. My determination to remain positive and upbeat for my son began to droop. I wanted to escape into the fresh air, to get away from the reek of depression.

A glance at my watch showed I had twenty more minutes to wait before my number would be called and I could see my son. I had arrived at the Medford, Oregon, jail at 6:30 A.M. on a foggy spring morning and had stood in line with twenty-five sleepy men, women, and teenagers. Weary-looking adults pulled along small children as they proceeded in line to a window to get a number. On some Saturdays and Sundays, I had waited two to three hours to get to the front of the line. Usually I went alone. A friend or two would sometimes go with me for support, but I selfishly preferred to have the precious twenty-minute visit with my son all to myself.

At my first visit, some weeks earlier, I experienced the first shock of seeing Rodger garbed in a dull-gray, poorly fitting jumpsuit. His hair was closely cropped, his beard was gone, his eyes were tired and troubled. I had gradually grown accustomed to his changed appearance, but not to the ache in my heart and the yearning to hug him and assure him that everything would work out all right. Aware that our conversation was monitored, we talked through phones on either side of the glass that separated us. It was always difficult to leave him and walk out into the freshness of a bright, new day.

On the way home from the jail on that Saturday morning, I stopped at Lithia Park in our town of Ashland. I got a refill for my coffee thermos at a stand near the park and walked until I found an empty bench on a quiet, sunny pathway. Despite the peaceful beauty of the park, I was beset with a sinking, almost guilty feeling. How could I enjoy the tranquility of the park while my son was shut away behind brick walls in a hostile, threatening environment? Like countless times before, I began to wrestle with the big question: How could this tragedy have happened?

Our nightmare had begun several years ago when Rodger had been accused of "indecency with a child." I painstakingly reviewed the past years. What could have been done differently? How could Rodger's lawyer have erred so seriously in his advice to plea bargain? For the thousandth time, I could come up with no real answers. The pressing issue became: How could I help my son meet this unexpected and unwelcome challenge with courage, faith, and confidence? How could I help him keep his spirits up? How could I do the same for myself, not allowing my usually strong faith to be overcome by emotional devastation? And how could I help my compassionate son—who would never even kill an insect, but remove it from the house to continue its life—cope with this confinement?

The questions continued, along with a sense of futility and deepening fear. I had faced many challenges in my nearly eighty years of life, including a serious bone disease when I was a child, the anxiety of having my son David in the Vietnam War many years ago, a mastectomy at age seventy, and the dissolution of a fifty-three-year marriage. Then there was the more recent move to a new state, constant knee pain and impending surgery, and the challenge of finding meaning and purpose in my senior years. But it all paled in comparison to this stress of Rodger's imprisonment.

I had hoped that my senior years would follow a happy stereotype. I had dreamed of retiring with more than a comfortable income, experiencing the joy of a dependable marital relationship, and having happy, successful children and grandchildren living nearby. Now, here on this park bench, life seemed to have fallen into irreparable chaos. The dream was not as I had planned it. In spite of my years of praying for my children—for their success, their safety, and their spiritual growth—something had gone terribly wrong for my firstborn. And our whole family was affected.

It was in 1993 when our world began to unravel. Rodger was on one of his twice-yearly treks through the Southwest and then to Florida. He was speaking and giving workshops in a variety of New Thought churches—those connected with Unity or Religious Science and similar groups. He traveled in his ancient Volkswagen bus, enjoying the long off-the-freeway routes, reveling in the scenery and freedom of going at his own speed. Along the way, lodging and meals were provided for him in homes of church members. The trip was going well, and Rodger was touched by the hospitality shown him in the various areas he visited.

In a small Texas town, Rodger was housed in the home of a single dad with a five-year-old daughter.

Rodger has always been good with children. With his original stories and ability to draw children out with a song or joke, he has been appreciated by both children and their parents. On a Saturday evening, Rodger began playing with the daughter, tossing the little girl, who was wearing jeans and T-shirt, into the air and catching her. I had seen Rodger do this many times with his own children when they were small. Rather than catch them under their arms, which hurt them, he would catch them with one hand on their chest and one hand under their seat, and let them down gently. Her smiling father looked on. After the little girl went to bed, Rodger chatted with her father before they both retired for the night.

Six months later, Rodger was arrested at his home in Moscow, Idaho, for charges brought against him by the little girl's mother. She had never met Rodger but was maintaining that her former husband was entertaining an undesirable man in his home. The ex-wife's apparent motivation was to gain custody of her child. Her husband, who had said he would not testify against Rodger because it wasn't true, disappeared for reasons we never knew, and he could not be found.

In ensuing months, Rodger made eighteen trips to Texas for trial. Each of the first seventeen dates was cancelled after he had made the four-thousand-mile round-trip. We hired a highly recommended attorney who, on the eighteenth trip, told Rodger that he would never get a fair trial in Texas but would get at least a seventeen-year sentence. After a few moments of consideration, as jurors gathered in an outer room, Rodger agreed to a plea bargain. This was much against his instincts and mine, but the lawyer was insistent. (He later confessed to us that it had been a bad bit of advice.) The plea bargain document, signed in November 1995, called for three years of probation. Rodger was told he would be notified when his probation period began. He headed back to his home and his life in Idaho, and to wait to hear from them. The plea bargain document had been mailed and was waiting for him when he arrived. In it were several harsh, binding conditions that had been added after he signed it.

Rodger never received instructions about his probation, although he phoned his attorney frequently. Apparently no news was good news. In the spring of 1996, as my knee condition worsened, Rodger came to live with me in Oregon.

With the assistance of friends, Rodger and I started the Center for Positive Living, a New Thought church in Ashland. Skilled in computer work, Rodger took care of many details of the new ministry. He spoke frequently on Sundays, provided music, handled the sound system, and was in charge of children's activities. The kids adored him, and so did their parents. He also performed weddings, filling in for me when my knee problem made walking difficult. He was a tremendous help around the house—carrying in groceries, gardening, and providing a sympathetic ear as my pain worsened. My other son, David, a commercial artist, had moved to Oregon and lived nearby, and my daughter, Ann, moved from the big island of Hawaii to help me. We had some precious time together, with Rodger's and David's sons spending holidays with us when possible.

On a cold November day in 1997, almost exactly two years after the plea bargain was signed, two Ashland policemen appeared at our door and announced that Rodger had been on probation since June 1996, a move about which he knew nothing, having had no word from his lawyer or the courts in Texas. He began a probation program in nearby Medford at once. He spent several hours each week in sessions with a probation officer, who once commented to me, "Your son is in denial, but we can take care of that. I will break him in ninety days." I hastily and probably unwisely replied, "You may break his body, but you will never break his spirit."

Part of Rodger's probation included mandatory group sessions in which participants were required to write narratives of acts of sex abuse, many of them made up to satisfy the examiners, who read them and commented on the writings. One day Rodger stood up and said, not for the first time, "I am not guilty and do not belong in this group." The probation officer retorted that such denial constituted a violation of probation, and Rodger was thrown in jail. After five weeks there, with no hearing, he was flown to Texas and kept in a holding area, twelve-by-fourteen feet, with forty men. There was little food, scant water, and inadequate facilities. When I learned of these conditions, my heart ached. How could such squalor exist in the United States? The description sounded more like a Third World prison. The feelings of helplessness and futility were overwhelming.

Again, we hired an attorney. There was a hearing to review the charges against Rodger concerning the violation of probation. The attorney was ready to present evidence that Rodger had complied with the requirements for probation, but the court did not allow it. The probation officer, flown to Texas from Oregon, stated before the judge that Rodger had not completed his probation time, was not rehabilitated, and therefore deserved a prison sentence. The judge immediately sentenced him to eight years in prison. Case dismissed.

Rodger was then sent to another Texas prison and has been moved three times since then. His parole date, for good behavior and work time served, was set for August 1999. Then, just before that date, it was changed for no apparent reason to September 2001.

I flew to Texas several times through the financial help of a friend to whom I will always be grateful. It was wonderful to tell Rodger how much he is loved and how people all over the country and in other parts of the world are praying for him. We talked about our family and had a few tearful moments as I told him of the memorial service for his father, who had passed away just a year prior. (I had asked permission to have Rodger come to California to take part in the service, but the Texas authorities did not allow it. In fact, I had to notify Rodger of his father's passing through a letter, as a phone call was not permitted for that purpose.)

During my visits, we resolved to continue to put our trust in God and to write about some of the lessons we'd learned throughout this colossal challenge. It is our deepest hope that our readers might in some way benefit from Rodger's insight, written from within prison walls.

Share Your Problem
with Someone You Trust

"A sorrow shared is a sorrow halved."

—Shakespeare

When I heard the pinched tone of my ex-husband's usually jovial voice on the phone, my heart began to pound. "Sit down, Marg. I have some very bad news. Rodger has been arrested for indecency with a child . . . something they say happened six months ago in a little town in Texas. Charges were just filed by the child's mother."

I was conscious of a choking sensation, a struggle to breathe, as he continued, "We have to see about a lawyer right away. He has to appear in court in Texas in a week. You'd better call him right now." With that, the phone went dead.

Dead describes the way I felt as I placed the phone in the cradle . . . numb, unbelieving. The rest of that night is a blur, but I do remember that before I dialed my son's number in Idaho, I hurried to the apartment next door to seek out my best friend and mentor for the past forty-five years. Grace had seen my family and me through some challenging times, and her unfailing, confident reassurances that God is in charge, no matter what the problem, never fails to comfort me. As I knocked on her door that night, I had the hopeless feeling that Grace's inner tranquility would be wasted on me, that this problem was too big even for her limitless resources of insight and strength. I was wrong.

After receiving Grace's calm assurance that God was still in charge, I phoned a dear friend who has been close to Rodger all his life, one whose spiritual strength and wisdom would become a reliable ally in the uncertain days ahead. Crying, confused, and probably rather incoherent, I poured out my fear and grief and felt steadiness and a strange kind of calmness take its place.

When trouble strikes, whatever the nature or degree of the problem, our first inclination is to share it with someone who will understand. The feelings of loneliness, abandonment, and vulnerability are almost overwhelming. It is, therefore, vitally important that we share with someone who is nonjudgmental. We need someone who can be objective enough to offer the kind of support we need without getting involved in all the details, one who will not "preach" and be swayed in their loyalty by what we are telling them. Such friends are rare treasures. Fortunate are you if you have such a one in your life.

If you don't, get in touch with a minister, rabbi, or spiritual counselor. If you do not have a spiritual connection (church, synagogue, or other religious affiliation), ask around for a recommendation. Be sure the channel of your spiritual support has a positive, loving, nonjudgmental philosophy. You don't need sanctimonious do-gooders who will point out that you are learning an important lesson through this problem. That may be very true, but first you need strong, loving, affirmative interaction with an individual, fellowship, or group that will remind you of your inner courage and strength, that will support you in your efforts to live and grow through this difficult challenge.

You might also call your local mental health agency. They will refer you to state- and county-sponsored services that can connect you with local support groups, not necessarily spiritual, but psychologically based and operated by trained, qualified personnel.

If possible, establish a prayer partner relationship with someone you feel is spiritually sound and empathetic with your needs. Such a person might be a member of your church, a caring neighbor, a spiritual teacher . . . someone who loves you unconditionally and will listen to you with respect and patience. Arrange a mutually convenient time to connect in prayer, a time when you can both set aside all distractions and simply abide in the awareness of God's love and provision for you. Elaine, a friend of mine in another state, has shared with me her painful journey of adjustment since the death of her husband, followed just a few weeks later by the accidental death of her only daughter. When she called to tell me of the tragedies, I suggested that we join together, she in her home in Utah, and I in my home in Oregon, to hold a "tryst" each day, an appointment with each other and with God. We agreed on the time of 5:30 A.M. Oregon time, 7:30 A.M. her time, and for the past year we have kept this commitment. For fifteen minutes we read the same page in a devotional book that we both love, and we pray for God's peace and comfort to flow into her mind and heart, dissolving all sense of emptiness and loss.

Sometimes one of us will call the other and then we have the advantage of hearing the other's voice and sharing some special answer to our prayers. We have not seen each other in years, but the bond between us is not dependent on physical sight or contact. We are bonded in our love for God and in our mutual trust in His perfect plan for our lives. We have both discovered that another person can help us see our problems from new angles.

When we confide in compassionate, positive people, our spirits are lifted, our perspectives are expanded, and the present that looked horrible yesterday, or five minutes ago, doesn't seem quite so black now. It is the same world, but when we change our thinking about it, we change the way it affects us. If you do not have such a friend, keep your eyes, ears, and heart open. There is such a one, and your need and desire will bring you together.

Rodger adds:

During times of stress, it is vitally important for us to do everything we can to buoy our spirits and prevent them from being dragged into the mud and muck of sorrow, fear, frustration, and dismay. Other people can help us see our problems from new angles. When we confide in compassionate, positive people, our spirits are lifted, our perspectives are expanded, and the present that looked horrid yesterday doesn't seem so bad today. It's the same world, but when we change our thinking about it, we change the way it affects us.

Today there exist countless support groups, prayer groups, and discussion groups made up of people who have been through some of the same challenges. The people who attend these groups know how important it can be to share problems, to have someone to talk with. We are social creatures for the simple reason that we live better together than alone. We are in other people's lives so that we may help each other over the difficult times that are part of every human experience.

Face Facts, Tell the Truth, Have Faith

"Acceptance of what has happened is the first step
in overcoming the consequences of any misfortune."
—William James

"Prepare for the worst, expect the best, and take
what comes."
—Robert E. Speer

It can be difficult to talk about a family member's imprisonment. We often fear criticism and judgment. News of an alleged criminal deed on the part of a family member can cause friends to become uncomfortable and even disappear from our lives.

Our first hurdle of disclosure came after Rodger was suddenly placed on probation in Medford. He was no longer allowed to assist me in the ministerial duties of our Center for Positive Living, including working with the children's program. I announced the situation to the adult congregation while Rodger explained to the children that he needed to take some time away from them. Parents comforted their children by telling them that Rodger would possibly be back with them sometime in the future.

To digress briefly, for the past ten years I have mailed out a monthly newsletter to some five hundred people throughout the world—former colleagues, people who had been part of the church I pastored in southern California, and friends from speaking tours I had taken around the world. When Rodger came to live with me, I frequently mentioned his helpfulness and support in the newsletter. When he was sent to prison in Texas, however, I suddenly refrained from mentioning him. Some readers called or wrote, asking about him. I simply replied that he was out of the state for the present. I longed to tell the truth but felt obliged to comply with a desire of my ex-husband to keep the information in the family. When I did ultimately relate Rodger's imprisonment in one of the newsletters, the response was quick and strong. Countless friends wrote, "Why didn't you let us know so that we could help in some way?"

Local friends who found out about Rodger's imprisonment were also quick to offer encouragement. Many phoned or dropped by. Prayer groups in many parts of the country called to say that they were praying for Rodger. I gave special thanks each time someone, usually a stranger to me, phoned to say that they were part of a prayer group in a church where Rodger had spoken during his ten years of itinerant ministry. They wanted him to know that they loved and respected him, no matter what the appearances and charges were. I was relieved that the word was out and people were praying.

The biggest test in the matter of disclosure of Rodger's imprisonment came when his father passed away in 1999. Our family gathered for the large memorial service—the only absent members were Rodger's older son, who was on a world tour with other college students, and Rodger. I announced in the course of the service that Rodger was "away and could not be with us, but his love is very much a part of this service." Out of respect for Rodger's father's wishes, I gave no further explanation, and many people who had known Rodger all his life looked puzzled. People who later learned of Rodger's whereabouts were eager to extend their concern and support.

Yes, there were some people in our town who promptly dropped any contact or connection with us. It hurts to have trusted friends desert us, but I have come to value even more the many friends who have stuck by us and who have supported us in our efforts to have Rodger released. We learned that when we reached the point of talking about Rodger's situation openly, most people were understanding and helpful. Trying to keep a situation quiet can take time and energy away from finding solutions.

There is another important facet of this complex issue of facing facts. Granted, we need to accept the reality of what happens in our lives, but we must also recognize that attitudes can change facts.

Charlie, the son of an acquaintance of mine, was convicted of a serious drug charge and sentenced to fifteen years in prison. Charlie's mother, Donna, was devastated. The evidence was irrefutable, and Charlie began his prison term.

After the initial shock, Donna resolved to do all in her power to reverse her mindset of tragedy, loss, humiliation, and hopelessness. She contacted her minister, who was eager to help her make positive changes. He believed, as I do, that our experiences are strongly affected by our thoughts and that facts can be altered by a changed heart and mind. The church's prayer group began at once to pray for Charlie and his family.

Donna spent time each day reading inspirational literature and meditating on her strong belief that "all things work together for good to those who love God" (St. Paul). She began to find ways to love God more than she had ever done before. She faced the facts of the present moment—her son was in prison and wrote heartbreaking letters about the conditions there. They couldn't readily change those circumstances, but they could change the way they looked at the situation.

Donna did not write to Charlie of her personal project of changing her own attitude. She *did* write cheery, newsy letters about their family and gently urged her son to read motivational, inspirational books that she ordered sent to him from a local bookstore. She was supported emotionally and spiritually by friends who believed in the power of prayer to change things.

Donna discovered that prayer puts us in tune and in harmony with God's will for our lives. It moves us from a place of preoccupation with our problems and opens us to the possibility of new solutions. We might say that prayer lifts us from the level of the problem and places us on a new, higher level where we find acceptance, answers, and peace.

By her change in attitude and reliance on prayer, Donna was able to inspire and support Charlie through her letters. He caught the essence of what was happening, explored some possibilities for further education, and signed up for a computer class offered in the prison. He made regular visits to the prison library, and his letters became much more positive in tone and content. Charlie is still in prison but is eligible for parole earlier than expected. This is partially due, I believe, to the strong, positive energy of love and faith on the part of his mother and all those praying for his highest good.

My son is also still in prison. It was difficult to accept the fact that his expected parole date was postponed for another two years, but that is where our faith comes into action. Since we have prayed about his situation for years, we can only assume that there must be some higher purpose fulfilled by Rodger's imprisonment. I believe that much good is being accomplished by his calm, compassionate presence in dorms where the prevailing mood is tension and hostility.

On one occasion, Rodger was threatened with physical harm if he did not "pay up" to a small group of inmates who discovered the charges against him. He had no money except the modest amount I send for stamps, paper, pencils, and coffee. Certainly the amount would not satisfy extortionists.

Rodger refused to fight and, although he was very frightened, he tried not to give in to the fear. He breathed deeply and tried to pray for the angry men and to feel the divine protection that is always with him. Several other inmates witnessed his courage and came to his defense. The bullies backed off and were soon moved to another dorm.

A fact, just as real as Rodger's incarceration, is that he is making a difference in the lives of other prisoners. I am filled with pride and gratitude for the privilege of having such a son—sentiments I express to him often in letters.

Rodger says:

It is profoundly traumatic to be publicly vilified or to live through the hurt and anger when this happens to a loved one. Under such trauma, our normal modes of thought and action are thrown awry, the solid ground under our feet turns to mud, and we're no longer sure which direction is up.

As will be discussed later, all challenges arrive in our lives not to punish or reprimand us, but because they bring lessons that we are ready to learn. Nothing can happen to us that is beyond our ability to handle. Nothing happens by accident—everything has a purpose.

To discover the messages and lessons that are woven into our experiences, it is vitally important to be realistic about what is happening. We need to be careful not to ignore or sugarcoat an issue for fear of judgment or disapproval from friends or family. To effectively deal with a situation, we have to perceive the truth of it. We can't fix an airplane and make it airworthy again if convinced that it's a bulldozer.

A wise person once remarked that the shortest path out of a problem is through it. Evasive and wishful thinking are never helpful. When we are brave enough to look the problem in the face and see it for what it really is, our fears tend to diminish. Like a fog that has rendered us blind, our worries are greater than the problem. Seeing the facts is the first step in overcoming an obstacle.

Imprisonment carries with it a great many value judgments. We must be careful not to take these judgments as facts. We must know our own truth and not be swayed or intimidated by the rumor or innuendo that inevitably swirls around those who are singled out for criticism. We must accept the facts of a situation without also accepting the emotional baggage that comes with them. Perhaps the facts of imprisonment are unjust or the punishment much worse than the crime. But until fairness, proportion, honesty, and accountability play a larger role in our process of justice, we must accept the realities and hope for the best.

The sooner we reach the point of accepting things the way they are, the less energy we will waste in living an illusion, and the more energy we will have to cope and to create change.

One Day at a Time

"To me, every hour of the light and dark is a miracle,
Every cubic inch of space is a miracle."

—Walt Whitman

As long as I can remember, I have planned ahead and taken pleasure in having something to look forward to—a trip, a visit to friends, a special dinner, a concert. These events were like carrots dangling in front of me, adding zest and a sense of expectation to life. In my work as a minister, careful planning was essential, and I delighted in putting together a six-month schedule of sermon topics, projects, and activities.

Unfortunately, I also had grandiose and sometimes unrealistic expectations for my children. All three of them were great kids and gave their father and me little cause for concern as they grew up, but that wasn't enough for me in those days. I expected them to love church as much as I did, which didn't always happen. And I felt let down when they made choices that weren't the right ones from my viewpoint. It was difficult to remember that they were spiritual beings living on Earth for the purpose of expressing their own natures. I needed to have frequent reminders that they came with their own agendas and had a right to make their own decisions and live with the results of those decisions. In short, I was a master planner—and I thought that others should conform to my plans.

Eventually a phone call changed all that. One moment, life was relatively serene and predictable; the next moment, everything was up in the air when I learned of Rodger's legal trouble. Gone were my great expectations, for it seemed foolish to make plans. A call in the night—perhaps a new development in Rodger's situation—could change everything. Trips were cancelled, and I stayed close to the phone, dreading what might be more discouraging news. My "carrots" were gone.

I remembered one of the discussions Rodger and I had had a few months previously. He said, "Mom, most of your frustration and unhappiness comes because things don't turn out exactly as you expect. You have high hopes for Ann and David and me, and that isn't wrong, but you and Dad also raised us to think for ourselves, to be responsible for our decisions and actions." He looked at me for a moment, as if making sure that his remarks hadn't hurt my feelings. "You try to plan things for us and get us to see things the way you see them. But in spite of the fact you obviously have more experience than we do, we aren't necessarily going to do things your way." He laughed and added, "How about some iced tea to cool down this heated discussion?" He leaned over and planted a light kiss on top of my head, saying, "Because you and Dad are opposites in many ways, you contributed some diverse characteristics to us kids, but we're glad you got together and did that."

Remembering that conversation, I now make a conscious effort to avoid too much planning, either for myself or for others. I've learned that the best-laid plans sometimes have to be abandoned at a moment's notice. Rodger's freedom and homecoming are examples. We have been disappointed many times when we thought that event seemed imminent. When I realized how much emotional energy I was expending when things didn't happen according to my timetable, I began to change my perspective.

I have begun to practice "being in the moment" and seeing each day as an "airtight compartment," as one spiritual teacher used to term it. He advised, "Live each day as a whole and complete experience. Determine first thing in the morning that you will be conscious and aware of everything around you, of all that is happening to you. Take time to smell the roses and take time for several acts of kindness during the day. Live the day as if it were the last one of your life, and at the end of the day, you will know that it was worthwhile."

I would add this recommendation: Each morning, open your eyes with the words, "God bring into my life this day those to whom I can be a blessing and who can be a blessing to me." Some nights I find myself wishing I had never said it when the day has been full of people with problems. Then I remind myself that I asked for it and, in retrospect, the blessings far outweigh any inconvenience.

I would like to suggest another simple practice to you, my friend. Before you fall asleep at night, ask yourself three questions about that day: Did I love?

Did I receive love? Was I of service? Elisabeth Kübler-Ross, the noted authority on death and dying, says that we are presented with these three questions when we die. So wouldn't it be wise to ask ourselves these questions now? Since I began this practice, I haven't had a single boring day. Some days are more pleasant than others, of course, but they are all valuable in terms of being a blessing to someone. And because what we give out comes back in some way, we reap countless rewards.

When we live in daily airtight compartments, neither worrying about the future nor regretting the past, we can live with serenity and faith. When my faith is tested and I tend to become fearful about the future, I remember a favorite quotation by Ralph Waldo Emerson: "The things I have seen teach me to trust the Creator for the things I have not seen." I pause often to recall the countless times I have experienced God's love and goodness and how many seemingly terrible situations worked out for the ultimate good.

I remember the time when I was scheduled to fly to the East Coast for a convention where outstanding metaphysical leaders would be speaking. I had my ticket, was packed, had all the lists and provisions ready for the friend who was staying with my family, when one of my sons came down with a bad case of the flu. How do you tell a sick little boy that mom won't be around for a week when he needs her so much? I couldn't. So I unpacked, refrained from telling God what I thought of this development, and settled down into my usual routine—fixing dinner, reading bedtime stories—and also making phone calls canceling hotel and airline reservations. I went to bed that night feeling very sorry for myself, and my prayer time was pretty short and curt, I'm afraid.

Two days later, my son was feeling better. The crisis was over, but I was still terribly disappointed at having missed the long-awaited conference. The phone rang, and it was a friend from the past, a dear, much-loved friend whom I had not seen for years. She and her husband were in town on business and we arranged to meet for lunch the next day. What a treat that was! She had news of other friends I hadn't heard about in years, she brought me a new book which became one of my favorites, and that night I prayed a prayer of thanksgiving and decided that in the future I wouldn't question God's sudden interference in my plans. He always has our best interests at heart.

I recall the difficult time right after the death of my ex-husband. The "ex" category had existed only a few months, and the marriage had lasted fifty-three years, so the pain of separation was sharp. My son was, by that time, in prison, another son lived nearby in Oregon but not with me, and my daughter was happily settled in a great job and a beautiful home in Hawaii. I was really alone for the first time in my life, facing a serious knee surgery and a long convalescence. The future looked empty and a bit frightening, when my daughter gave up the life she loved in Hawaii, moved to Ashland, bought some acreage in a lovely area outside of town, and made arrangements for me to have a manufactured home on her property. She took over all the legal matters, got my affairs in order, gave me a home while mine was being constructed, and today I can happily say that things have worked out better, more harmoniously and comfortably than I ever imagined they would. So I am a believer in God's plans for our lives when we give Him a chance to carry them out and do not doubt, argue, and resist.

All of these experiences have caused me to ask, "Why should I think anything is too hard for God? Haven't I placed my beloved son in His care, knowing that He loves him even more than I do, and that He has a divine plan for his life? This difficult experience must somehow be preparation for what Rodger is to do with his life. This is all part of the divine plan." This kind of self-talk lifts me out of depression and impatience, and I feel renewed faith and trust. Then I go about the day, appreciating the beauty around me in the rolling hills of Ashland. I find new energy to pray for others, write a note of encouragement, or make a phone call to someone who is ill.

Another practice I've adopted is turning the whole day over to God, knowing that I'm being guided and protected in ways that are for my highest good. I see my son going through the same process despite the crowded, noisy, sometimes hostile conditions of prison life. I visualize him reading the books he loves, doing his prison job, sharing a kind word or smile with a fellow inmate who is despondent. I envision Rodger as ever conscious of the inner light—a spiritual power often known as the Christ consciousness—that never leaves him and is available whenever he calls. I see that light permeating his cell, moving through the hall and other cells, and touching inmates, guards, and visitors.

I find that when I focus one day at a time and make the most of that day, I live with zest, joy, and trust. My son, too, is affected when he senses my new confidence. My friend, I hope some of these ideas will work for you too.

Rodger adds:

When one is in prison, one is said to be "doing time." Surely the loved ones of the prisoner are also doing time, since imprisonment affects not just the accused person but everyone to whom he or she is connected. The duration of our sentence is the time we must do.

But the phrase "doing time" is true in another sense, too. With so much time to fill, we are probably spending a large amount of it thinking about the past and the future. This can be a destructive trap.

When we think about the past, we open ourselves up to the endless rehashing and reliving of events. We think of the things we could have said and done but didn't, and we can become angry, frightened, and frustrated. Likewise, when we dwell on the future and ponder situations that might occur, we often experience a wide range of negative emotions.

Science has shown that when the imagination entertains a train of thought—the recollection of an argument, for instance—the body responds as though the argument were currently happening. Feeling upset—whether from real physical circumstances or anticipation of them—evokes the production of adrenaline, which the body dumps into the bloodstream for immediate use. If there is a snake coiled before us, ready to strike, this adrenaline provides the necessary energy to jolt us into moving out of striking distance. If the snake is an imaginary one, however, the adrenaline will still quicken the pulse and increase blood pressure. The result is destructive to health, just as gunning a car without engaging the transmission is not good for the engine.

When our thinking is not distracted by past and future, all our faculties are available for the present. This is what it means to live life to the fullest, regardless of circumstances. The past and future take us away from the "now." Spiritual teachers throughout history have recommended being in and remaining in the now. Through the practice of focusing on the current moment, the future has a way of working out as it's supposed to, the way it would if we weren't incessantly trying to control it. It's this effort at control that leads to many of humanity's problems.

Love Unconditionally

"Love never empties your heart, nor giving your hand."
—Calendar

"Someday, after we have mastered the winds, the waves, the tides, and gravity, we shall harness for God the energies of love. Then for the second time in the history of the world, man will have discovered fire."
—Teilhard de Chardin

A friend recently remarked, "It's one thing to be loyal and supportive when you know the one incarcerated is innocent, when you believe in him or her completely, but it's impossible for my family to stand by my brother-in-law. He's as guilty as can be. How would you deal with that?"

My friend Jan and I were having coffee at a sidewalk café in Ashland. She had phoned just a few hours before, saying that she needed to talk with someone about the stress in her family since her brother-in-law was charged with robbery, convicted, and sentenced.

"He's still a part of your family," I responded. "You said he's a good husband to your sister and a great father. Yes, he made a serious mistake in judgment. Bear in mind that he will not receive affirmation of himself as a worthwhile person while he's in prison. As Nelson Mandela knowingly wrote:

Prison is designed to break one's spirit and destroy one's resolve. To do this, the authorities attempt to exploit every weakness, demolish every initiative, negate all signs of individuality—all with the idea of stamping out that spark that makes each of us human and each of us who we are.

I continued, basing my words on what I had observed through letters from a number of inmates who had been with Rodger at some point. "The motivation to change, to 'mend one's ways,' as my mother would have expressed it, just isn't there. It must be supplied from people outside appealing to the innate divinity that exists in everyone regardless of their circumstances. That motivation must come from family and friends who love the person unconditionally."

As I spoke, I was reminded of a lesson I had learned during years of counseling with hundreds of troubled people and one that served me well in dealing with problems in my own family: Learn to separate the doer from the deed. Many times, in raising our three children, I had become angry or upset over an action or a decision. But I eventually discovered that no matter what the deed, my love for the child was not altered. He or she was still my beloved child; my love was not dependent on anything that he or she might or might not do. There was great emotional freedom and peace of mind in that realization.

Jan concentrated on my words and then said, rather hesitantly, "Yes, I can see some truth in what you say, but you are a minister and have to practice what you preach. Besides, you believe in your son's innocence. How would you feel if you knew he were guilty?"

Just then Jan's husband approached our table and, after a polite nod to me, informed her that he was double-parked in front of the coffee shop. She jumped up, put some money on the table for our coffee, patted my shoulder, and said, "Thanks for the help—guess I have a lot to think about. See you soon."

After Jan left, I ordered another cappuccino and reviewed our conversation. How would I feel if I knew that my son were guilty of the charges against him? I would hope to be able to turn from accusation, disappointment, and judgment and allow my love to flow unimpeded. I would hope to be able to support him and love him unconditionally, as I was doing now. It would be his family's love, not criticism, that he would need the most.

My mind flashed to a day months earlier when I kept an appointment with a highly recommended astrologer whom I had asked to prepare Rodger's birth chart. In my search for answers, I made it a policy to follow every possible lead.

The pretty, blonde woman with the incredibly blue eyes looked briefly at the chart she had constructed. Smiling, apparently confident of the news she was going to share, she said, "Well, my dear, this is some offspring that you attracted into your life. First of all, he should work with children. He has a natural affinity for and with children. He knows how they think and is expert in communicating with them. He should be a teacher—can be a tremendous influence for good in the lives of children. He should also . . ."

I interrupted her, rather rudely I'm afraid, by blurting out, "So why is he in prison for indecency with a child? How could this happen? And what can be done about it?"

The now troubled-looking woman across the desk frowned and replied, "I don't know your son but would be willing to bet that the charges against him are false, that he could not be guilty of such charges." She continued in a more positive tone, "I can say this with absolute certainty. The whole mess will end in light, and many people will be helped in the long run. Keep the vision before you of all he is and all he can be. Try to convey to him your confidence and belief in him." She shared more information of an optimistic nature, and in the following days I often reread her written report for encouragement.

I think of minister Chuck Swindoll's "ABCs of Love": "I *accept* you as you are. I *believe* you are valuable. I *care* when you hurt. I *desire* what is best for you. I *erase* all offenses."

Unconditional love. It changes people—both the giver and receiver. And it can make a huge difference in the lives of our loved ones behind bars.

When Life Seems to Hit Rock Bottom

"I believe in the sun even when it is not shining,
I believe in love even when I do not feel it,
I believe in God even when He is silent."

—Scrawled on the basement walls of a
German house in World War II

I am well aware that, believing as I do in my son's innocence, I might have difficulty putting myself in the place of those whose situations are far more serious and in some cases almost without hope of solution. I have prayed about this and asked for guidance as to how I might helpfully meet the needs of those who face a bleak future.

As part of my morning preparation for the day, I ask that God send into my life that day those to whom I can be a blessing. I am getting used to surprising answers to that prayer. I was deep in sleep at 3 A.M. one morning, when my bedside phone rang and a weak, female voice on the other end said, "Please forgive me for calling at this awful hour, but I live on the East Coast and have to leave for work in a few minutes. I just had to try to reach you." The shaky voice continued, "My friend, Bette, lives in Ashland and she told me about a book you and your son are writing and she thought maybe you could help me. I don't want to go on living. My life and the lives of my family are completely shattered. My husband has been convicted of a terrible crime and sentenced to life in prison." By now she was sobbing so hard I could barely make out her words. I gently told her to slow down, get a drink of water, take a few deep breaths, and continue when she was ready.

She was silent a few moments; then, obviously under a bit more control, she continued her sad story. "I just don't see how I can go on. We have three teenage children and they have to live with the scorn and rejection of their classmates at school. The story has been in all the papers. Our lives are ruined. I love my husband and want to do what I can to make his life in prison more bearable, but what can I do? And how do I deal with the pain and shame my kids are having to endure?"

Suddenly I was faced with a bigger challenge than I had asked for, a need I felt totally inadequate to meet. And yet, hadn't I asked God to send into my life those to whom I could be of help? God doesn't make mistakes, and He must somehow know that I could help her.

She told me some more particulars about her husband's plight, and while she was talking, I thumbed through a national directory of metaphysical churches and ministers in her area. (Another example of serendipity—that directory belonged on my desk in another room . . . why was it on my bedside table that night? I am still puzzled by that one!) The directory contains names and addresses of ministers of metaphysical churches that believe and teach material similar to what I believe and have taught for more than thirty years. I searched for someone who could contact her that very day and offer some kind of immediate assistance. I found the name of a former colleague whom I had met at a church conference years earlier and with whom I had corresponded for a short time. I knew this man to be a compassionate person and prayed he would welcome my call with its urgent request to help this hurting wife and mother.

The troubled woman, Lola, was now calmer, and I briefly told her that I would be in touch with my friend, the minister whose church was in her small town. I didn't promise anything, of course, but told her I would see if he could find someone to talk with her in person. Then I asked her permission to pray with her right then and there. She quickly agreed and I silently asked God to put into my mouth the words that would bring her a measure of comfort and peace. I don't remember what I said but knew that God was speaking through me. I believed that my deep desire to heal her intense pain was the intent God would use to start the healing.

I got Lola's phone number and offered to call her that evening when she got home from work. Then I began to pray that my minister friend could be reached and that he would respond to my request for help. Even though it was still pitch-dark, I got up, made a cup of coffee, and read some pages from one of my favorite books, *The Quiet Mind*, by White Eagle. An hour or so later, I dialed the number listed for my friend in my directory. Praise God! He answered and was surprised and seemed pleased to hear from me. (I hoped he would be just as pleased when he heard why I was calling.) He couldn't have been kinder and more understanding. He took the information and promised to get in touch with Lola that very evening.

When he called me late that night, he reported that he had seen Lola in her home, visited a few minutes with her hurt and angry children, and made inquiries about seeing her husband in prison. He had also very thoughtfully made arrangements for the service organization in his church to assume the responsibility of seeing to some of Lola's material needs.

Since that first nighttime conversation, I have spoken with Lola several times. I write to her every ten days or so, sometimes sending a book or tape that she can read or listen to for spiritual support when circumstances seem overwhelming. She tells me that just knowing there are people who care makes all the difference in the world. Her new friends in the church are practicing the universal teaching of unconditional love and compassion that all great religions embody. Her children are now part of the youth group and have found friends who accept and welcome them. In one of our conversations, I suggested that she start seeing her husband on a regular basis, remembering what my few visits to my son meant to both of us. Her husband is located in a facility not too far from their home, and although the round trip takes most of a day, she has started going every Saturday, often taking the children with her. Her husband can't help seeing the remarkable change in his wife's attitude and demeanor, and that encourages him to make the best possible use of his limited existence. He is taking some courses in electrical engineering and also attends a study group sponsored by a local church. Even though he is faced with a life sentence, he is learning about spiritual principles that transcend human experiences. He is determined to do his best, beginning to believe that miracles still happen when one's total faith is in God and His divine purpose.

I mentioned reading some passages from a favorite book, *The Quiet Mind*, as I waited to call my minister friend on the East Coast. Later, when I corresponded with Lola, I felt strongly led to send her a copy of this simple little book. Now she loves it and finds the same, comforting inspiration that has fed my soul for so many years. One quotation from the book is especially appropriate here.

It may comfort you to know that every one of you who undergoes some experience involving pain and anguish, and which might be described as a crucifixion, is doing something for the whole world; for anyone who meets such testings of the soul in the same resolute and tranquil spirit (in however small degree) as did Master Jesus, is helping to quicken the vibrations of the whole Earth. Whatever your occupation while in your physical body, remember, it is a form of service. However humble or even humdrum your work may seem to you, it is your special appointment, and through your work on Earth you can make your contribution to the happiness of all. Work hand in hand with God, and be thankful for every opportunity to serve which lies before you. One soul can help the whole world. You say, "I want to do some work. Use me. Here I am." But my child, you don't need to come to Me to offer yourself. The service is there beside you, and waiting in your own heart every day. The greatest service that anyone can give is continually to think aright . . . to continually send forth love, to forgive.

(White Eagle 1972)

A few months ago, I attended a conference of metaphysical churches and groups, an organization with which I have been involved for more than thirty years. At that gathering, I heard a young woman sing a song that touched my heart deeply. With her cocomposer, Jason Blume, she writes songs about her life, her mother who has Alzheimer's disease, her independent teenage daughter, and how she is able to meet her challenges with faith and courage. She sings with such feeling and depth that one cannot help being moved by the lessons she shares with her listeners. I called and asked for her permission to use the lyrics of one special song, which is included on one of her sensational CDs. She kindly agreed. Her name is Karen Taylor-Good, and these are the words of "What I Need" from her 1999 album, *Perfect Work of Art:*

I knew all the answers, the way my life should go,
And when I used to say my prayers, I would tell
God so.
It seemed He wasn't listening. I thought He
didn't care,
But lookin' back, it's plain to see that He was
always there.
'Cause I prayed for strength and I got pain that
made me strong.
I prayed for courage and got fear to overcome.
When I prayed for faith, my empty heart
brought me to my knees.
I don't always get what I want. I get what I need.
I'm not sayin' that it's easy, or that it doesn't hurt,
When nothin' seems to go my way, nothin'
seems to work.
But these days I'm gettin' better at goin' with the flow,

Accepting that sometimes the answer to a prayer
is "no."
Every time I've had a door slammed in my face,
In time a better one was opened in its place.
I don't always get what I want. I get what I need.

My friend, I do not have any convenient platitudes
that can erase the kind of suffering experienced by my
friend Lola or that you may be undergoing right now.
I can empathize with you. I can yearn, deeply, to
lessen your pain, to give you some of my faith. I can
believe in your innate power to overcome this tragedy
in your life and in your family's life . . . and I do, all
of these. I have seen so many seemingly impossible situations completely reversed when there is a change of
heart from abject hopelessness to faith in a loving God
who always wants what is for our highest good.

As spiritual beings living in physical bodies and a
material world, we are given free will, and sometimes
that freedom allows us to make unwise choices that
result in conditions we deplore, but we cannot blame
God for our foolish decisions. God, in His infinite wisdom and love, takes our apparent mistakes and uses
them for some good purpose. Nothing is lost in God's
universe. No failure is final; no mistake is permanent.
God's incredible love, which created us and sustains us
through all the ups and downs of earth living, will
never forsake us, but is as near as our breathing and just
as real. You can know that you are safe in that love, no
matter what the appearances to the contrary might be.

I once had a teacher whose favorite statement was,
"There is only God. All else is a lie." The great metaphysical teacher and prolific writer of transformational
books, Joel Goldsmith, had one pivotal principle upon

which he based all of his teaching and healing ministry, a work that covered the globe. It was, "God is
the *only* power." If we could really believe that statement and live as if we believed it, our lives would
change for the better in the twinkling of an eye!

Why Do Bad Things
Happen to Good People?

"Penetrating so many secrets, we cease to believe in the unknowable. But there it sits nevertheless, calmly licking its chops."
—H. L. Mencken, American essayist

"Accept that some days you're the dog and some days you're the hydrant." —Unknown

Why do good people suffer? Although this subject has long intrigued me, it was not until my son's imprisonment that I felt compelled to find answers.

I cannot approach this question without stating that I am a believer in the principle of reincarnation— the idea that we have all lived many consecutive lives in different locations, different color skins, different cultures. On the surface, this concept may seem far-fetched, but a thorough study of the subject can bring a sense of the order and harmony of seemingly random events.

Before you decide to avoid this discussion because it goes against your particular religious beliefs, or your church doctrine frowns on it, or for some other reason, please read on. The following ideas may make sense to you and help you deal with this thorny question of why bad things happen to good people.

My introduction to reincarnation came many years ago when my second son developed a speech difficulty at about four years of age. My husband and I took David to speech therapists, doctors, and psychologists, all of whom offered partial answers based on their particular field of expertise. We read books on child psychology and took seminars and classes, but nothing seemed to work. Then a friend suggested that we contact a woman in Los Angeles—a deeply spiritual person who reportedly had a remarkable ability to look into people's past lives and find causes for current challenges. Somewhat skeptical yet hopeful, we contacted her and arranged for a "life reading" for David.

I could write a book about that experience and its effect on our lives and on David's. This insightful, sensitive, and caring woman brought to light information on David's previous life and some of the emotional events that might have produced his speech problems in this life. She spoke of events, dates, and people that she surely could not have fabricated. My husband and I left her home that evening with some answers that made our parenting easier and more effective. And, as a result, David's speech began to improve.

Reincarnationists view life as a continuous process, with each soul—the "real" person inside the body—experiencing many births and deaths. This process of encountering the polarities of earth living—joy and sorrow, success and failure, comfort and suffering, victimizer and victim—is necessary for the evolution of the soul. The soul advances and learns with each life, eventually realizing its oneness with God. This advancement is the purpose of earth lives.

At the center stage of reincarnation is the law of karma, which is simply the law of cause and effect. The principle states that for every effect we experience in life there is, somewhere, at some point in time, a cause. The cause could occur in this life or in a previous one. The law of karma also teaches that like attracts like. What we give out in thought, word, or deed sooner or later returns to us. If we've harmed others, we can expect to eventually experience negative consequences, although perhaps not until a future life. If we've been kind, we can expect to eventually experience positive consequences. Because of the possible time lag, many people don't understand this cause-and-effect process and think they can lie, cheat, steal, etc., without consequence. The law of karma tells a different story, however. It teaches that perfect justice exists and that no one ever gets away with anything.

What does this have to do with understanding why good people suffer? To put it simply, we do not know what events from past lives are contributing to the circumstances of this one. We do not know what causes may lie behind the effects we see happening today. We do not know what lessons the soul is working on this time around. But we may be assured that there is a reason and a higher purpose behind every occurrence— seemingly good or bad—that we experience. And it's all happening to make us better than we were when we came here.

Many years ago, when I was minister of the Santa Anita Church in Arcadia, California, I cherished a yearly ritual of going into the beautiful, inspiring sanctuary early each January 1. I'd watch the sun come up over the San Gabriel Mountains and illuminate the church's magnificent Tower of Light and the entire place of worship. I was sure of being undisturbed, since everyone was at the Rose Parade or sleeping in after a night of revelry. For many years I maintained that practice, and each time I asked for guidance for the coming year. Should I focus on harmony in the congregation? Expansion for the children and youth programs? More abundance and financial security? More courage and faith to meet the challenges that were so much a part of church leadership?

One bright winter morning, as I sat in the front pew, asking, waiting expectantly, I heard a voice inside my head. Now, I don't usually hear strange voices! But that morning there was no question that something, someone, was speaking to me. The voice said, "Remember that nothing can ever happen to you that is not for your highest good." I immediately thought of some difficult times the church had experienced during the past year and challenged that idea, but the voice came again, louder this time, repeating the words. After a few moments of pondering that strange message, I returned home, but the words continued to echo in my mind. They echo still, and I can honestly say that as I look back over the past, everything has worked for good, as Paul the Apostle promised in his immortal statement, "All things work together for good to those who love God . . ." (Rom. 8:28).

I now see how Rodger and I have both grown in our understanding and acceptance through his imprisonment. I do not see the whole picture, but that is where faith comes in. I recall the many experiences, disappointments, setbacks, and delays that have chipped away at my faith but not overcome it. In retrospect, I see that every one of those deterrents ultimately brought about some good, some change for the better. It may have taken months or years, but the good did materialize. And with each demonstration, my faith deepened. The ultimate good of this current concern is not yet apparent and might not ever be apparent to us in this life, but I believe it is coming about in God's time and God's way. And our souls will be the better for it all.

My daughter-in-law, Lois, a nurse, has questioned the suffering deaths of children, families watching the deterioration of loved ones, and the gallant but vain fight that many wage against cancer. Telling me of these heartaches one day, she added, "We don't care for the concept that we are powerless over some aspects of our lives, but I've seen people experience deep, positive changes as the result of facing difficulties. It's the test of the mettle of the people involved as to how they cope and grow (or not) from these experiences. I've concluded that there is no one absolute answer."

Rodger adds:

We wonder how it can happen that good people sometimes get clobbered with negative experiences. And when life slips us a blow-out at the least convenient time, how quickly we point accusing fingers at the tire, the dealer, or the highway department.

Indeed, we would never stop to ask this question if our world views were accurate. We ask this question because our understanding of life has some serious holes in it. In the words of the popular song, "When you point your finger 'cause your plans fell through, you've got three more fingers pointing back at you." Discovering the existence of such holes is the first step in fixing them.

As children, we were all aware of a sense of fairness. It emerged in us so early that it is tempting to consider it a natural tendency. When young, we demanded, as much as we were able, to be treated fairly, and our outrage was acute when we felt we'd been cheated. Few of us ever outgrew the expectation that balance and proportion ought somehow to be facts of life whatever our age or circumstance. So we immediately feel that something is seriously wrong or somebody must be seriously at fault whenever unfairness or injustice impose themselves on us.

To justify and support our expectations of life-long fairness, most of us endorse some form of what is called the law of cause and effect, which seems to provide a mechanism—almost an algebraic proof—whereby balance and fairness are considered to be built right into the system of how things happen. Perhaps for you the law wears the Judeo-Christian garb of "an eye for an eye" or "as you sow, so shall you reap." For those who are not so "Occident prone," there is the Oriental equivalent, called karma, generally understood to be the running balance of so-called good and bad deeds for which we are certain to be compensated. Whichever version we espouse, it seems perfectly natural, if not deadly certain, that good people would lead lives lavishly furnished with wonderful things and conditions, while bad people would accordingly reap punishment for their dastardly deeds. Speaking religiously, we all pretty much assume that one of God's main occupations is seeing to it that the good guys are rewarded and the bad guys are punished.

So, it comes as a real challenge to our understanding when really bad things happen to really good people or when really good things happen to the jerks and the bullies. Our concepts of justice and fairness are strained to the breaking point to account for these apparent anomalies, so we must resort to escape clauses to preserve our preconceptions: we identify, then blame the devil for our ill fortunes, we conclude that God must be testing us, or we invent reincarnation to extend the period of moral accountability over several lifetimes when the karmic sums for just one brief lifetime don't add up. Our religious and philosophical systems grow ponderous and self-contradictory until we don't know what or who to believe.

Our confusion is the result of our shortsighted views of reality, our propensity to judge and jump to conclusions when our egos are unwilling to live with the unknown. We rush to label everything; that way we can manipulate labels—which is easy—instead of the realities behind those labels—which isn't easy. Labels will always mislead, regardless of the authority under which they are issued or assigned. Labels are judgments.

Perhaps you have heard the parable of the wise old man with the son and the beautiful horse. The king, having heard about the fabled horse, offered the old man a fortune in gold for it. But the old man politely declined the offer, saying that he couldn't sell the horse, since the horse was his friend.

The next day, the horse was missing from his stall, and the neighbors chided the old man, saying, "You were a fool not to sell that horse while you had the chance. Now you have neither the horse nor the gold." The old man reserved judgment, saying, "Let's wait and see how it turns out."

The next day, the horse returned, with a bevy of mares. The neighbors said, "Oh, how fortunate you are, for now you have many horses, and the prospect of many more." The old man just smiled.

The next day (in parables, everything happens the next day), while breaking one of the horses, the son was thrown to the ground and suffered a broken leg. "Oh, how unlucky," consoled the neighbors, "for now you must handle all those horses by yourself." The old man remained silent.

The next day, the kingdom went to war, and all the able-bodied young men were conscripted into service . . . but not the old man's son. And so it goes . . .

At each turn of apparent fortune, the neighbors were only too happy to lend their expertise in judging the succeeding developments, but the wise old man knew that everything in the world of phenomena changes, and that what is called bad today may very well be called wonderful tomorrow.

When we label something as good or bad, right or wrong, and especially when we seek to assign blame and punishment based on those labels, we are judging. In this modern world of near-phobic litigiousness, we do a lot of judging, don't we? By doing so, we blatantly ignore one of the simplest yet most important of Jesus' messages: "Don't judge." There is no blame when judgment ceases. What is simply is, with no credit or blame whatsoever.

Where my personal prison experience is concerned, I tried everything. I played the victim. I sought legal redress. I looked for and found people to blame for putting me down and keeping me there, including myself. I looked for something I might have done for which this could be payment. I tried to see it as a lesson to be learned, a challenge to be surmounted, a karmic debt to be paid. I tried on every explanation I could find to make sense of it, but nothing really clicked.

But then I realized that maybe there is no divinely ordained fairness to be maintained after all. For God lets the sun shine and the rain fall on saints and sinners alike. Maybe it really isn't helpful that we try to affix blame or cause to the things that happen to us.

Maybe instead of blaming the tire or the dealer it makes more sense just to change the tire and get on with the trip. Maybe the best answer to this question is also deceptively simple and straightforward. Why do bad things happen to good people? Just because . . .

Forgiveness, the Great Healer

"Life is an adventure in forgiveness."
—Norman Cousins

Suddenly being thrust into the role of family member or friend of a prisoner can be a shock. One day, life is relatively uncomplicated. The next day we are plunged into a world of fear, uncertainty, anger, and often a sense of being a victim.

We focus on the glaring questions that keep returning like a tape that is stuck on a reel. What went wrong? What awful thing have I or my family done to warrant this tragedy? We also tend to blame others for the situation—the accuser or law enforcement or the criminal justice system.

From the moment of my son's arrest, in addition to my concern about what lay ahead for him, I was consumed with feelings of anger and frustration. I eventually had to deal with the emotions that were destroying my peace of mind, my sense of perspective, and even my health.

My anger was first directed toward the mother of

the child, who, never having seen Rodger, had seemingly used him to accomplish her own selfish purposes. She seemed to have no regard for how her action would affect him and his family. I considered writing to her, begging her, mother to mother, to ponder what she was doing to her own five-year-old child, who was being relentlessly questioned by social workers. I wondered how she could disregard the results of her blind and thoughtless accusation.

One night I read some passages from *A Course in Miracles*. After begging God to show me something that would help ease the pain in my heart, I ran across these words: "Every act of evil or unkindness is a cry for help, a cry for love." I asked myself how that mother must have felt when she decided to accuse my son of indecency with her child. Was it fear of losing the little girl in the custody battle with her estranged husband?

I then thought of another person who had been the source of much pain and fear. That person was the probation officer, who from the beginning of his association with Rodger had seemed intent on breaking him down, forcing an admission of guilt. One afternoon this man sat in my living room, smiling, remarking on the pleasant surroundings. Then he seemed to change suddenly—to become the tough cop. It was then he told me, "Your son is in denial, but I will have him broken in ninety days." My defiant reaction to his words seemed to strengthen his determination to prove me wrong. From that day on, his treatment of Rodger seemed ruthless and uncompromising. During the past two years, the probation officer has surfaced several times to reassert his opinion, resulting in further delays in a parole date, and ultimately a prison sentence of eight years without benefit of a trial or hearing of any kind. It has been a severe test to be on the receiving end of prejudice, vindictiveness, and seemingly unwarranted hostility. There were days when I had to work hard on my own attitude, to keep from wishing that something awful would happen to him, that he would suffer for his actions.

The subject of anger, while not a pleasant topic to discuss, is a big part of the prison experience, for the prisoner and the family. Anger is a natural response to injustice. It is an emotion that needs to be acknowledged and addressed. If left to grow and flourish, it can be a real factor in ill health, both physically and mentally. It does not just affect the person who is fleeing the anger, but since energy follows thought, it goes out into the world with its negative, destructive vibrations and affects countless others, who, in turn, pass it along to those with whom they come in contact.

Jesus' example of anger, throwing the money changers out of the temple, is one of the few stories of this man of peace ever giving in to righteous indignation, but it is important to note, I believe, that his anger was not based on what had been done to him but rather was directed toward those who were using the holy temple for fraudulent, personal, greedy purposes. Later, at his crucifixion, with the worst, most heinous, actions being perpetrated against him, he was able to forgive his tormentors, a demonstration of his spiritual stature that few people since have been able to emulate.

I must admit to surprise and chagrin when I found myself actively hating and wishing hurt and pain for those who put my son behind bars. I thought about and rehashed in my mind the wrongdoing of the legal system that never gave him a chance. The ill-considered advice of his attorney to plea bargain. Being imprisoned for denying his guilt to the probation officer. At the probation hearing his attorney not being permitted to present proof that Rodger had indeed followed the probation requirements. Since 1993, three denials of our requests for appeal. Two top-notch lawyers, dispatched by a generous friend, went to Texas for three days to study Rodger's case. "This man has been framed from the beginning," they reported. They also found many inconsistencies and unconstitutional actions, including locking up Rodger for saying he was innocent. They suggested we appeal his case on the federal level, but that appeal would cost an estimated three hundred thousand dollars . . . and there was no guarantee an appeal would be granted.

Anger welled up inside me just at the thought of the guards who stood by while he was being attacked by a few angry fellow inmates and verbally abused with vile remarks such as, "Think you're safe, white boy . . . just watch your back." (I learned of this incident from a fellow prisoner who is now free.)

Feelings of frustration and helplessness were almost overwhelming. For some time, anger kept me in a very personal prison of bitterness and, at times, even rage. Suddenly I saw what these emotions were doing to me and what they were doing to my son. My bitterness and anger colored the tone of my letters to him, fueling the fire of his own desperation and despair.

About that time, someone gave me an article about a Dutch Catholic priest and his incredible example of forgiveness during the horrible days of Dachau. This saintly man was subjected to hideous physical experiments, which eventually led to a welcome death. His last words, spoken to the attendant who injected him with the fatal shot, were words of forgiveness and blessing.

I remembered a conversation Rodger and I had one time when I visited him in prison. I had just poured out to him my anger at the guards who had stood by, callous and unconcerned, and watched him being abused by the troubled inmates. Rodger, with his usual calm, objective manner, replied, "Mom, they are just doing what they have been told to do. Most of them have a very limited education, and they grew up in a community of people who have lived in this small town all their lives. They are not bad people, just limited in their perception of the larger world, of other and better ways of dealing with people. The pay isn't that great, they have personal worries, financial and with relationships, and many of them are frustrated and unhappy in their jobs. They walk out of here at night, but they are not free." He looked around the room and pointed out the guards, some of whom were more humane and considerate than the others, and he continued, "You know what to do, Mom. Pray for them. You know that the energy you have been putting into hating them can be directed in a positive direction. You know that better than I do, Mom," he added with a grin and a pat on my hand. "Turn on the love spigot and let love flow from your heart to everyone who needs it so desperately. You'll be more at peace, and only God knows what good can come about because of your better use of your energy and intention."

I was telling about that little episode in a talk I was giving for a local church recently, and later a frowning woman came up, pushed her way through a small group of people gathered around me, and blurted out, "How can you forgive the people who do awful things to your son? You should be sticking up for him, not praying for his enemies." She looked around, as if expecting nods of approval, but there were none. I took her hand and said, "I forgive because I need forgiveness and I can't expect to get it unless I give it. If you would like to talk further about your question, please wait a few minutes and we can visit." Without a word, she turned and disappeared into the crowd. I felt sad, because I would have liked to have helped her. She was obviously in pain. Anger and ill will do that to us.

For more than thirty-five years, I had been giving sermons and talks on the topic of forgiveness and thought I was well acquainted with the subject. Wrong! The current demand for forgiveness became a new lesson, a new opportunity to know the full meaning and significance of the word. Several spiritually supportive friends began to mention forgiveness and to drop off books and articles on the subject. At first I wasn't open to any of their efforts to help, just didn't want to discuss the subject. After all, my son was the victim of a vicious allegation, a captive of a harsh, punitive criminal justice system. The more I dwelt on that thought, however, the more hopeless and dejected I felt. Finally, I picked up one of the many forgiveness books stacked on my desk and reluctantly began to read.

Two of the books became my almost constant companions. One is *Forgiveness: The Greatest Healer of All* by Dr. Gerald Jampolsky, and the other is *The Twelve Steps of Forgiveness: A Practical Manual for Moving from Fear to Love* by Paul Ferrini.

I suggest that you read the Jampolsky book once through to glean the simple but extremely effective principles and results of practicing forgiveness. The one-liners in each chapter are worth writing down. Post them in various places around your home where they can inspire you throughout the day. Some examples from the book (Jampolsky 1999) are:

> "We can choose to have peace of mind as our only goal."

> "We are responsible for our own happiness."

> "Forgiveness means seeing the light of God in everyone . . . regardless of their behavior." (Wow! That's a great one, but not easy to accomplish.)

> "To be happy, all I have to do is give up my judgments."

You get the idea. Just one of these statements, considered thoughtfully and practiced often, can change your life and the life of the one you want so much to help.

After you make a consistent diet of these transforming ideas for several days, slowly and thoughtfully read Dr. Jampolsky's entire book. It is filled with down-to-earth suggestions for making forgiveness a daily practice on all levels of human experience. The book also contains many moving stories of how forgiveness has healed broken lives, mended fractured families, and restored individuals to health. I have nearly memorized the book, and it goes with me everywhere. When waiting in a doctor's office or for the tea water to boil, I welcome Gerald Jampolsky's wisdom and insights as my companions.

Dr. Gerald Jampolsky has very kindly allowed us to

use this remarkable poem as a part of this book and suggests that it be read weekly as a way of reviewing some of the forgiveness principles found in his valuable book *Forgiveness* (1999):

> To forgive is the prescription
> For happiness.
> To not forgive is the prescription
> To suffer.
> Is it possible
> All pain
> Regardless of its cause
> Has some component of
> Forgiveness in it?
> To hold on to vengeful thoughts
> To withhold our love and compassion
> Certainly must interfere
> With our health
> And our immune system.
> Holding on to what we call justified anger
> Interferes with our experiencing
> The Peace of God.
> To forgive
> Does not mean
> Agreeing with the act;
> It does not mean condoning
> An outrageous behavior.
> Forgiveness means
> No longer living in
> The fearful past.
> Forgiveness means
> No longer scratching wounds
> So they continue to bleed.
> Forgiveness means
> Living and loving
> Completely in the present

Without the shadows of the past.
Forgiveness means
Freedom from anger
And attack thoughts.
Forgiveness means
Letting go of all hopes
For a better past.
Forgiveness means
Not excluding
Your love from anyone.
Forgiveness means
Healing the hole in your heart
Caused by unforgiving thoughts.
Forgiveness means
Seeing the light of God
In everyone, regardless
Of their behavior.
Forgiveness is not just for
The other person—but for ourselves
And the mistakes we have made
And the guilt and shame we still hold on to.
Forgiveness in the deepest sense
Is forgiving ourselves
For separating ourselves from a loving God.
Forgiveness means
Forgiving God and our
Possible misconceptions of God
That we have ever been
Abandoned or alone..
To forgive this very instant
Means no longer being
King or Queen of the Procrastinators' Club.
Forgiveness opens the door
For our feeling joined in Spirit
As one with everyone
And everyone with God.

It is never too early
To forgive.
It is never too late
to forgive.
How long does it take
to forgive?
It depends on your belief system.
If you believe it will never happen,
It will never happen.
If you believe it will take six months,
It will take six months.
If you believe it will take but a second,
That's all it will take.
I believe with all my heart
That peace will come to the world
When each of us takes the
Responsibility of forgiving everyone,
Including ourselves, completely.

Here is one more thought-provoking idea I found in a collection of inspiring quotations:

A human being is part of the whole that we call the universe, a part limited in time and space. He experiences himself, his thoughts and feel-ings, as something separated from the rest—a kind of optical illusion of his consciousness. This illusion is a prison for us, restricting us to our personal desires and to affection for only the few people nearest us. Our task must be to free ourselves from this prison by widening our circle of compassion to embrace all living beings and all of nature.

—Albert Einstein

Paul Ferrini's *Twelve Steps* (1991) also contains a wealth of helpful ideas for moving out of condemnation and judgment into the much more comfortable realm of tolerance, forgiveness, and acceptance. A quotation from *A Course in Miracles* opens the book: "Trials are but lessons that you failed to learn, presented to you once again, so where you made a faulty choice before, you now can make a better one, and thus escape all pain that what you chose before has brought to you." In his book, Ferrini gives four axioms of forgiveness and twelve clear steps to take to move from fear and misery to forgiveness and peace of mind.

Have you ever thought, as I once did, that with age comes a release from having to work hard at having qualities like forgiveness? I identify with the story of the grandmother who was seen every afternoon in her rocking chair on her front porch. One day, as her small grandson came by with his school friend, the friend asked, "Why does your grandma sit there every day, reading her Bible?" The grandson replied, "She's crammin' for her finals."

During the past few years, I've felt like I, too, am crammin' for my finals. I am experiencing more spiritual growth and more joy in the spiritual journey than at any other period in my life. Much of the growth has to do, I believe, with forgiveness . . . going through the intense but healing process of forgiving the people involved in my son's imprisonment—the accuser, the probation officer, lawyers, judges, and guards. I thought my job of forgiveness was nearly complete, but I found out differently at a small gathering of friends in my home one evening.

During our conversation, I mentioned that I was preparing for another trip to Texas to visit my son and made a mindless declaration. "I dread entering that state again. I dislike everything about it—the climate, the flatness of the land, the attitude of some of the people. . . ." Susan, a friend whose spirituality shines forth from her face, said quietly, "Well, Margaret, you know that part of your forgiveness practice must extend to the state itself, to the people, and to the government." I knew that she was right.

Susan continued by telling of a recent trip to New York City to visit her daughter. She had never driven in the city but rented a car and asked for divine protection. She felt that protection around her like a cloak as she drove on crowded streets in fierce traffic, eventually arriving safely at her daughter's home. She admitted that New York City was not a place in which she yearned to live, but on the day of her return flight, she bought a special mug in an airport gift shop. It read "I Love New York," and when she got home, she placed it in a prominent spot in her kitchen. Each time she sees it, she is reminded of her safe, pleasant trip to the city. Doors of welcome and opportunity had opened to her because she expected them and was sending out love and appreciation for New York.

You may not see a cup saying "I Love Texas" in my kitchen, but I am taking Susan's gentle advice to love the state, the people, and the weather, and to expect a pleasant and fulfilling experience when I next go to see my son. It feels good to have that hard lump in my heart dissolving, to know that the enemy is not Texas. I believe that all aspects of my next visit to Texas will be blessed because of a simple change in attitude.

Rodger comments:

It seems to be a part of human existence that situations and circumstances arise over which we seem to have no control. It is a waste of energy to blame others (even though "finger-pointing" is still zealously practiced by the courts, the press, and many churches). These circumstances— challenges, really—can make us or break us, depending on how we choose to react to them. We have a choice of basically two ways of responding: we can take the low road or we can take the high road.

The low road is the way of anger, hatred, retribution, vengeance, and other negative responses that people often adopt in answer to the "slings and arrows of outrageous fortune." The Old Testament way of "getting back" at those who did us dirt—an eye for an eye—is still the modus operandi of the legal system. Unfortunately, this approach perpetuates the very iniquities it claims to relieve. As Martin Luther King, Jr. said, "An eye for an eye leaves everybody blind."

A desire for revenge creates stresses that can be physically devastating to an individual. Anger, resentment, and spite can eat at our internal organs like battery acid, resulting in cancer, heart disease, and all manner of physical breakdowns.

The high road, on the other hand (or maybe the other cheek), uses these stressful and trying experiences as springboards to a greater and deeper understanding. We are forced to search for a deeper meaning in existence. We may read books we wouldn't otherwise have touched or seek perspectives of people we formerly ignored. Eventually we discover new insights that begin to make sense.

I was accused by someone I never met of doing something I didn't do. I paid a lot of money to a lawyer who never helped me in any meaningful way. I was never tried for the accusation but rather was declared guilty by a judge who sided with the prosecution at every turn. The only testimony allowed was presented by a probation officer who had boasted that he would "break me" but failed. On the basis of his testimony, I was sentenced to eight years in prison for my first offense of any kind. Consequently, there are several people alive today for whom I would be seemingly justified in feeling rage, hatred, and a burning desire to get even.

If I were to take the low road and succumb to those violent emotions, I would soon work my body into a state of permanent decrepitude. Society is no longer structured in such a way that we can quickly settle disputes "the old-fashioned way," so those emotions would eat like acid at my internal organs. My sleep would be fitful, I'd have nightmares, I'd be a physical and emotional wreck. And I might not live very long.

The alternative, of course, is to forgive people for the things they have done to put me here and keep me here. I can only conclude that their lives are already sufficiently miserable since they could so easily bring devastation to the life of a fellow human being. Sleepwalkers don't know what they're doing, and these people seem to be asleep to the truth of their realities. Can I blame a sleepwalker for bumping into me and knocking me over? No, I must become aware of their ignorance and forgive them.

Through forgiveness, I have freed up vast amounts of emotional and spiritual energy that now can be put to some positive purpose. Forgiveness is moving me light-years closer to understanding what life is really all about. Forgiveness helps me make the most of a bad situation and even turn it into something good for myself and others.

I have learned much in the prison experience, not the least of which is the realization that nothing can happen in this world without what we might call divine approval. I am here in this setting for reasons I have yet to discern, but the fact that I am here is unassailable. I must, therefore, assume that this is the best place in the universe for me to be, to learn and understand things that just wouldn't be possible in any other setting.

The next step in my learning is always right where I am. I needn't frantically search for answers. My responsibility is to focus on where I am now and do the things that today presents to me, living each moment as it comes.

This high road has led to perspectives I never could have envisioned before I was ready for them. Accepting their grace, peace, and truth has made all the difference.

Take Care of Yourself

"Above all things, reverence yourself."

—Ancient Greek Philosopher Pythagoras

I'd been speaking of some recent discouragement I'd felt over Rodger's imprisonment, and my good friend Pam looked at me strangely. Handing me a fresh tissue, she said, "I can't believe you just said that—you, of all people. You're a minister! You always seem to have a full supply of comfort for others. I've never seen you like this before, and it scares me." Pam frowned, dabbing at her eyes where tears had formed.

Pam continued, "I know you've had more than your share of problems lately, but you've always been so strong through them all. Get a grip. It isn't as if Rodger were dead or accused of murder or in a POW camp being tortured. You know where he is and that he'll be treated fairly."

"Oh, yeah?" I shot back. "Just a few weeks ago, he was threatened with physical harm and extortion by some bullies who found out the charges against him.

You read about these attacks in prison, but when they happen to someone you love, it's very real, and I felt totally helpless to do anything about it. By the grace of God and the support of a couple of guys who defended Rodger, he wasn't hurt. But he was afraid to turn his back or go to sleep. How can I not be a wreck?"

Breaking into fresh tears, I moaned, "I can't sleep. I imagine all sorts of horrible scenarios. I feel guilty when I sit down to a nice meal or watch the sun come up over the mountains." Then I whimpered, "I'll never be happy again." Even as I spoke, I knew that I was likely causing more misery for myself, for our words are powerful tools for creating our reality.

On the way home from the coffee shop where Pam had eaten and I'd pushed my food around on the plate, Pam asked, "When did you last see your doctor?"

"What's that got to do with anything?" I retorted. "There's no cure for a broken heart." But Pam made me promise that I would call for an appointment and insisted she would do it if I didn't follow through.

A few days later, my friendly young doctor sat at his desk looking at the results of some lab tests they'd completed. "Well, my dear, I have no really bad news for you. Your blood pressure is too high, but that is a problem we've been addressing for a long time. You are mostly stressed out, fatigued, and generally run down. You're going to need all the energy you can muster in order to carry on your church work and to be the support and lifeline your son needs now."

Then he proceeded to outline a simple, but to me rather ambitious, physical improvement program. I had every intention of carrying out his instructions, but there never seemed to be enough time in the following days, and I must admit to being lazy when it comes to physical exertion. In fact, I had always looked forward to the luxury of giving up physical exercise as I got older. It seemed acceptable to settle for extra pounds, less energy, and more excuses for avoiding increased responsibility. Surprise! It appears that the additional drain on my physical and mental resources for the past few years had changed that agenda. Now I knew that I needed to increase my fitness level in order to help my son, and in the process, help others that God was bringing into our lives.

This is another of the hidden blessings this experience is bringing to light—this added motivation to be well, to be stronger and more flexible in mind and body than I had been in years. With the dawning of this revelation, I got serious about improving every part of life, beginning with the physical. One day I drove five minutes to the local YMCA and signed up for a year of water aerobic classes for seniors. In addition to the water aerobics, I would have full access to the excellent equipment for cardiovascular conditioning. Our YMCA also offers interesting field trips with a vanload of lively seniors who are discovering some of the wonders of aging with grace and pleasure.

Of course, my new plan included more attention to a healthy diet, more raw foods, less coffee, a daily nap (one of the real blessings of retirement), and of course, the strengthening of mental and emotional health. Knowing the important connection between mind, body, and emotions, I am filling my mind with a more consistent diet of constructive, positive thoughts and ideas. For years, I have kept inspiring books in every room of my home, ready to be picked up for a helpful lift during a stressful day. I also make it a practice just before turning out the lights at night to read something inspiring and to write in my journal at least six things from that day for which I am thankful . . . a note from a friend, a welcome, surprise phone call, the gorgeous sunrise, the affection of my daughter's dog when he comes for his nightly turkey bacon treat, a comfortable bed with moonlight streaming over me as I sleep, and the growing confidence that God's will is being done in Rodger's life, no matter how things look. Going to sleep with such good thoughts seems to keep out the frightening, uncertain scenarios that sometimes try to come in the dark.

Another stress-reducer that I found important is humor. When low in spirits and convinced that nothing is working out as it should (as *I* think it should), it helps to take a break and see a funny movie or rent a couple of videos to watch at home with friends. You may remember Norman Cousins, noted journalist and author, who, during a life-threatening illness, was able to achieve two hours of pain-free living for every ten minutes he devoted to laughter. He watched old Marx Brothers comedies and the corny Three Stooges by the hour. He learned that laughter—hearty belly laughs— produced certain chemicals in the brain that benefit body, mind, and emotions.

Here is an appropriate story to give you a laugh right now. An elderly man and his wife found themselves at the Pearly Gates. They had been killed in an accident and arrived together at the door to Heaven. They were ushered in, shown around, and in no time were happily getting adjusted to their idyllic new life. There were old friends to greet them, wonderful food, a gorgeous home with all amenities, everything they could possibly want. They should have been ecstatic, but the husband turned to his wife, frowned at her, and growled, "If it hadn't been for you and your preoccupation with health foods and exercise, we could have been here ten years ago."

I also turned to music to reestablish a sense of well-being. Loud, discordant sounds produce stress, but harmonious, pleasant music calms the listener. My grandsons used to think I was weird and a bit unreasonable when, as little boys, they wanted to watch something violent, angry, and ugly on television but I insisted they change the channel to something pleasant and wholesome. They were too young to understand what they now know as adults, that vibrations are powerful vehicles for emotions and feelings. I didn't want my home full of discordant, disturbing, negative energies, and after the children and my home had been exposed to negative TV fare, I followed that programming with some good classical or light, popular music that cleared the air and established a feeling of order and beauty once again. These days, when I open a letter from Rodger, I first put on a tape or CD of calming, uplifting music as a backdrop for reading the letter.

During recent surgery when my right knee was replaced with a miraculous Teflon one, I chose gentle, inspiring Mozart tapes to be played in the operating room, believing they would have a soothing, calming effect on me as well as on the surgeon and attendants throughout the long, complicated procedure. Those particular tapes were recommended by a friend who has studied the effect of music on humans. Mozart tapes are available for mental stimulation, healing, help with school tests, and general well-being.

I have found other classical composers make valuable contributions to human conditions as well. When

I feel confused or distracted, the precision and orderliness of Bach's music is instantly effective. When there is a need to feel loved and secure, the choice is romantic Rachmaninoff tapes or something by Brahms. The music of Beethoven and Dvorsak seems to inspire courage and strength. But for pure comfort, peace of mind, and relaxation, Mozart is my favorite composer, and my home is filled with his music these days.

After I began taking better care of myself, my letters to Rodger became more upbeat. He had often advised me to eat right and get enough rest, and now I was following his advice. I found my normally high energy slowly returning, and I began to accomplish more each day and feel a greater sense of peace at night.

The situation my son faces is proving to be an incredible learning experience as I allow it to make me better, not bitter. The challenges are motivating me to keep strong and dependable, not only for Rodger, but for my family and friends and those who might need what help I can give them in the future.

Rodger adds:

Body, mind, emotions, and spirit . . . we can talk of these as though they were separate entities all thrown together like groceries in a bag of skin and bones. But, of course, they are not separate any more than red, shining, and juicy are separate components of an apple. As Alan Watts once remarked, "Mind is body looked at from the inside, while body is mind looked at from the outside." Body, mind, etc., are merely labels to identify different aspects of the whole person. "Sound mind in a sound body" was the advice of the Greek sages who understood that our minds work best if our bodies are healthy, and vice versa.

The stresses that accompany the prison experience are enormous, whether we are inside or outside the walls. Those stresses are largely ignored by those who impose them upon us, are glossed over in the statehouse and media, but are nevertheless profound. (Perhaps those who condemn people to such an experience would do well to have the experience themselves.) Unless it is relieved somehow, stress will begin to erode our health and well-being, weakening our resistance to disease and degeneration. Keeping our bodies in a healthy, exuberant state through nutrition, exercise, and getting enough rest will minimize the negative effects of the stress that the prison experience dumps into our lives.

Likewise, reducing stress by keeping ourselves in good mental and emotional tune will enhance our physical health. The process works in both directions—from the inside out and from the outside in. Taking good care of ourselves will enable us to more easily handle whatever comes our way.

Deepen Your Spiritual Roots

"God is life itself to us—the air, the bread, and the very blood of the soul. No one can live without, at every moment, drawing upon Him, however unconscious they may be."

—Unknown, as cited in *Truth Journal*

One of the most important lessons I have learned in my nearly eighty years on Earth is that we are part of an all-powerful, all-loving Being that created us out of itself and allowed us to come here to discover and demonstrate our divinity. This was not always my belief. I was brought up in a family where God was viewed as a stern judge in the clouds who knew everything there was to know about us. It was important to please this mysterious, unknowable Being. Unfortunately, most of the thoughts and actions that IT disliked were, in the human sense, the most fun.

During my preteen years, I battled a bone disease that was diagnosed as incurable. My father would sit by my bedside in the first anxious days of the disease and reassure me that I would walk again. He often moved my bed to an open window and arranged the pillows so that I could sleep with my head on the windowsill, feeling the breeze on my face. Gently holding my hand, he'd say, "Close your eyes now, honey, and pretend you're skating again. Remember how it feels to skim down the driveway on your new skates—how free and light it feels."

That was the beginning of my lifelong adventure in "acting as if," as championed by Shakespeare in his immortal words in *Hamlet*: "Assume a virtue, if you have it not." That simple practice was to help me through many difficult tests and challenges throughout my life, from walking despite the pain of my illness to, many years later, becoming calm and poised in front of a congregation.

The illness was also the beginning of changing my idea of God from stern judge to loving miracle worker. The bone disease went into remission after several surgeries on my right leg. Miraculously, it didn't spread to other parts of my body, as doctors had expected. My right leg, which had shrunk more than an inch in length, amazingly began to grow after my marriage at the age of twenty-three. The case was written up in medical journals and widely discussed by physicians.

Through my childhood illness and various other life experiences, I have come to believe in a loving, merciful God who desires our highest good. I believe that we all have a divine nature that expresses itself through us and manifests as health, supply, wisdom, love, truth, power, peace, beauty, and joy. I believe that our mental states strongly influence our reality through the law of cause and effect. And I think that our spiritual nature continues beyond the change called death. And oh, how I believe in the power of prayer.

It was easy to mouth these truths before a congregation, to utter words of comfort and reassurance to those in difficult situations. Then along came an event—Rodger's imprisonment—that challenged every belief I'd held. Where was God when my son was put in prison for harmlessly playing with a laughing, little girl? What good had been accomplished by those many years of praying for my children? To my dismay and surprise, I began to experience the deepest anxiety I had ever known. There were sleepless nights and frequent crying spells. I remembered comforting words I had spoken to grief-stricken parishioners—words and hugs that seemed to alleviate their pain. Had I really believed all those nice platitudes? Had they actually helped anyone? Why weren't those same words bringing me comfort?

Realizing that I needed to get back on track in my spiritual life, I dug out some favorite books that had been packed away in boxes. Several of them were exactly what I needed at the time, so I read them carefully, finding truths that I had overlooked in previous readings. I started to apply the various disciplines and practices that had been so much a part of my life as a minister. I phoned a dear friend, also a retired New Thought minister, and poured out my heart. It felt good to talk about the problem with someone who understood, who loved me unconditionally, and who had had her own share of challenges. In a gentle way, my friend reminded me of what I had been teaching all these years: Nothing happens by chance. There are no accidents or mistakes. There are reasons, though often not obvious, behind everything that occurs. And all of these occurrences help us to grow in faith, courage, and inner strength.

My friend helped me recall how many times my faith in a loving God successfully met some deep, serious need. As I began to gain a balanced perspective, the words of Kahlil Gibran came to mind. His essay on children in his classic book *The Prophet* (1946) had been almost like a Bible teaching to my husband and me during our early parenting days: "Your children are not your children. They are the sons and daughters of Life's longing for itself. . . . You may give them your love but not your thoughts, for they have their own thoughts. . . ."

My husband and I agreed that our children came to Earth by means of our physical union, but, as is true for all souls, were unique spiritual beings with their own agendas for life. We believed that Rodger, as all other souls, had chosen his path in every detail before he was born. He had made choices based on the knowledge of what it would take for him to fulfill his soul's purpose. He had been successful in a brief professional baseball career and highly successful in a business career, but it was always evident that his passion was helping people live happier, more productive lives. Perhaps after this time of imprisonment, he would be able to relate to people's problems and pain in ways he had never before been able to do.

When I was able to see a larger picture of recent events, my friend helped me put together a program of things I could do to stay in a positive frame of mind and in good spiritual health. First, I established a regular time each day to focus on the positive aspects of my life—a wonderfully loving and supportive family, good health for the most part, and my usually dependable optimism. I read a few pages each morning from inspiring books such as *The Quiet Mind* by White

Eagle, to which I referred earlier, and *Opening Doors Within*, a small book of daily readings by Eileen Caddy. I also read from Joan Borysenko's *Pocket Full of Miracles*, Neale Donald Walsch's *Friendship with God*, and Deepak Chopra's *How to Find God*.

After the reading time, I spend about fifteen minutes in silent meditation, visualizing the end of Rodger's prison experience—"seeing" him free and happy in his chosen work, enjoying his two sons and the beauty of nature in Oregon. (Important note: I stopped putting dates on my visualizations when I realized that God's timing is perfect but does not necessarily coincide with our human timetables. That was an important lesson for me.) I also imagine a ray of powerful, divine light flooding my being and flowing from my heart directly to Rodger's heart. This kind of mental imagery can have a powerful impact on our loved ones.

After this time of visualization, I spend another fifteen minutes in prayer for others. Then I decide on an affirmation for the day. (See the chapter "Affirm the Positive, Release the Negative.") This is a positive, uplifting statement such as, "God's love surrounds me," or "God guides me in all that I say and do." I repeat the affirmation several times with feeling and focus. Then I print it on several three-by-five cards and tape them on the bathroom mirror, kitchen windowsill, or on my computer, where I can be reminded and encouraged throughout the day.

Since I am an early riser, my daily spiritual practice can be accomplished before 7 A.M. If you try this plan, choose a time that works for you and adhere to that approximate time each day. You will begin to anticipate it as your appointment with God. Time set aside for this purpose will pay huge dividends in terms of peace of mind and can also strengthen your connection to your loved one in prison.

My attitude concerning my son's imprisonment has slowly changed from one of abject hopelessness to one of optimism and trust in God's perfect plan for Rodger's life. I have found great comfort in this statement: "God always has the last word and that word is always good."

My friend, this dark tunnel in which you find yourself *does* contain blessings for you and your dear one. Hold on. Have faith. Set aside spiritual quiet time. And allow God to work in and through your situation.

Rodger adds:

No matter what our age, occupation, or goals, we can always benefit by knowing more about spiritual principles. One of the best ways to do this is to read spiritual material.

By "spiritual," I refer to books, magazines, pamphlets, etc., that have as their theme the expansion of human awareness into the realm of the unseen. Spiritual material isn't necessarily religious. In fact, some religious material is more dogmatic than spiritual. Spiritual material increases our knowledge of divine principles and aids in our inner development.

All religious imagery and doctrine are best understood if taken symbolically. Conflict between religions and between sects within religions is generally the result of an insistence on interpreting religious scriptures literally. All religious material contains kernels of truth that can lead us to a deeper understanding and appreciation of our own divinity. But we must develop the ability to separate those kernels from the parts of the material that would shrink our consciousness and freeze it into a rigid knot of blind, fear-driven belief. We need to learn to eat the kernels but spit out the cob.

Spiritual material directly affects our thoughts. When we change the things we think about, we begin to see aspects of our existence that were previously unrecognized. Reality happens at many levels—not just one. Like the stations on a radio dial, all levels exist at once. Sometimes we are tuned to the lower end of the spectrum where fear, force, intimidation, blame, guilt, and shame prevail. Perhaps we don't realize that we can adjust our dial and tune to another station. If we never change our dial, not knowing that it's our God-given right to do so, it will seem that the world is composed largely of fear and force, etc. Reading and absorbing spiritually uplifting materials stretches our awareness and is an excellent way to change the dial.

Affirm the Positive,
Release the Negative

"You can either complain that rosebushes have thorns, or rejoice that thorn bushes have roses."

—Unknown

During the journey through the prison experience that you and your loved one are traveling, nothing is more important than your state of mind—your attitude toward what is happening. You will find that a depressed, negative, pessimistic state of mind will exert a negative effect on you, your loved one, and the outcome of the situation itself.

Our thoughts and words have a strong impact on how we feel. Perhaps someone asks you how you are feeling and you reply, "Oh, I feel awful—ache all over, tired, depressed . . ." Notice how you feel after such a statement—certainly not full of vitality and energy! Maybe at another time someone asks you how you feel and you answer, "I feel great—full of energy and enthusiasm—just wonderful!" Again, notice how you feel. There will be an improvement in your mood and how you actually feel after you make a positive statement.

Dr. Catherine Ponder is a remarkable woman who has helped change countless lives. She is author of sixteen books on the power of the mind and emotions. Her work deals primarily with prosperity and abundance, but the principles she teaches are universal. When applied to our everyday thinking processes, they produce amazing results.

Catherine is famous in the metaphysical, New Thought world for her skillful, practical use of affirmations. An affirmation is a positive, encouraging statement such as "God's love surrounds me," or "I am safe and life is abundant." When repeated frequently with emotion, affirmations can produce outer conditions that reflect their words.

Some months ago, Catherine sent a page of original affirmations, some taken from her books, others the result of the inspiration of the moment. I sent the affirmations to Rodger, who benefited immensely from them. He also passed the paper on to other inmates, who made rough copies to share with family and friends. I appreciate Catherine's thoughtfulness and generosity in allowing me to share them with you here. I pray that they will lift your spirits and set your thoughts on high.

By Divine Appointment

I am in the world by Divine Appointment.
Wherever I have been at any time in life, it has been by Divine Appointment.
Every place, every situation, every relationship has had its unique meaning and purpose. Every place I have been at any given moment was the right place for me at that time.

Every situation I have ever experienced has
had some magnificent purpose for me!
Every relationship I have ever known has
added new depth and richer dimensions to me.
Nothing has been by chance or without purpose, for the Spirit of God has been moving
throughout my life and leading me to this place,
this time, this situation, and this way of being.
I exist by Divine Appointment!
The place in which I live at the present is the
place I am meant to be for now.
The talents and abilities that I have developed
serve their perfect purpose for now.
God is the constant Presence in my life, and I
will always be in my right place, by Divine
Appointment.
I will always be in midst of the right experiences, by Divine Appointment.
I will always have wonderful people in my life,
by Divine Appointment.
I *live* by Divine Appointment.

—Dr. Catherine Ponder

My friend, speak these lines over to yourself several times. Do you feel the shift in your awareness, in
your attitude? No matter how difficult it is to accept
some of these concepts, realize that you are retraining
your mind to see things differently, to see them as they
really are, and to move from a victim consciousness to
a master consciousness. It *can* be done.

I suggest that you read about the life of Viktor Fran-
kl and his amazing transformation during his years in a
Nazi concentration camp. Read Nelson Mandela's story
and the equally surprising ending to his twenty-seven
years in prison. He is doing much good work now, not

despite his imprisonment but *because* of it. These people and many more have used their difficult years to grow in character, compassion, and tolerance. After their release from prison, they have inspired thousands of people. They may not have known of Catherine's Divine Appointment theory, but there is no doubt that they fulfilled a unique and important role in awakening the world to brotherhood and understanding.

Here are some of my favorite Ponder affirmations that I have "pondered" with success for many years:

"I now release and am released from everything and everyone who does not support the Divine Plan of my life." (I used this once to find release from a difficult and troublesome coworker. She took new employment, happily, and I replaced her with a pleasant, cooperative coworker.)

"I have time for everything that is a part of the Divine Plan of my life now." (This is a great one for getting rid of stress and finding time for all the necessary and worthwhile things that I want to do.)

"I praise the Divine Plan of my life, and I invite it to manifest so clearly and so plainly that I cannot mistake it." (I use this when I need clarity and discernment in making decisions.)

"The world is full of charming people who now lovingly help me in every way (and whom I now lovingly help in every way)." I love this affirmation that Catherine gave me many years ago. It was so useful and effective when I moved from one place to another and at first had little help. After this "magic affirmation," people seemed to come out of nowhere to give me a hand. It has worked every time for me, in most exciting ways!

"New, sincere friends and loved ones now enter my life and shower me with their goodness, as I shower them with my goodness." (Doesn't that give you a warm, cozy feeling? Maybe this one will bring some legal help you need or a new friend who will fill the empty place in your life.)

Experiment with writing your own affirmations about what you want to experience in your life. Read them silently or aloud several times each day. If possible, display them on three-by-five cards in your home or office. If someone questions you, tell them of your project and give them some three-by-five cards so they can get started on some miracles of their own.

I would like to suggest some reading material that can start you on the path to peace of mind and greater development of your understanding and acceptance of the mysteries of this thing called life. These books have become my daily companions. I read them over and over, each time finding some new gem of wisdom that carries me through the rough times.

The Relaxation Response by Dr. Herbert Benson (1975)
The Quiet Mind by White Eagle (1972)
The Power of Positive Thinking by Dr. Norman Vincent Peale
      (1952)
Love Is Letting Go of Fear by Dr. Gerald Jampolsky
      (1979)
Forgiveness: The Greatest Healer of All by Dr. Gerald
      Jampolsky (1999)
Opening Doors Within by Eileen Caddy (1996)
The Dynamic Laws of Healing by Dr. Catherine Ponder
      (1966)
(Or any of Dr. Ponder's other fine books)
Conversations with God (three books) by Neale Donald
      Walsch (1996, 1997, 1998)
(My favorite is his fourth book, *Friendship with God*
      [1999].)

There are many more, too many to list here, but you will be led to the ones you need at your favorite bookstore or library. Ask Spirit to guide you to the ones that speak to your heart.

I would like to close this chapter with a reading from *Opening Doors Within*. I read this particular one often and I feel God speaking to me:

> When one door closes, another one always opens. Expect the new door to reveal even greater wonders and glories and surprises. Always expect the very best from every situation, and see the very best come out of each one. Never become depressed or despondent as you see one door close in your face. Simply know that all things work together for good for those souls who truly love Me and put Me first in everything. Feel yourself grow and expand as you go through every experience, and look for the reason for it. Learn by it, and be determined never to make the same mistake twice, if you have made a seeming mistake, for much can come out of it when you do not allow it to get you down. Your whole attitude towards life is very important; therefore realize that life is what you make it. Make it a wonderful, joyous, exciting life where anything can happen at any moment because you are doing my will.

> (Caddy 1996).

Rodger adds:

> Have you ever seen the demonstration of resonance with tuning forks? The demonstrator— usually a professor-type in a bowtie and white lab coat—strikes a tuning fork, causing it to hum with a clear, monotonic ring. When another tuning fork of the same pitch is placed near the ringing

one, the second one begins to ring also, even though it wasn't struck. Because the two forks naturally ring at the same frequency, the one can induce a vibration in the other.

If that ringing tuning fork is placed in the midst of many different tuning forks, only those of the same pitch will pick up the vibrations and ring themselves; the rest will ignore the invitation. This is a demonstration of the principle of sympathetic resonance—a principle that allows radios and TVs to work.

This principle also operates in our lives. The emotional temperature of our thoughts is like the pitch of a tuning fork. Our thoughts, attitudes, and feelings are like the energy of the strike that sets the tuning fork to vibrating. The array of many different tuning forks is the variety and rich diversity of a world of potential that surrounds us. If we are vibrating with negative frequencies, feeling anger or hostility, then the energy of those vibrations activate circumstances in the world around us which, like the tuning forks, correspond to the frequencies we are generating. Even though all possible tones may potentially be there, we will be aware of only those that correspond to the thoughts in our awareness.

When we dwell on negativity, we'll experience negativity around us. Grouches use this as evidence that "life is a bummer, then you die." They are blind to beauty and wonder and the grand gifts that life can hold. They will claim, backed by the evidence of their senses and their experiences, that life is mean and cruel.

Prison is populated with and administered by people who are immersed in a negative viewpoint. They look to find fault wherever they can. It's a tremendous challenge to resist the temptation to surrender to the mass thinking, but it can be done and is well worth the effort. When we dwell on how lousy things are, then that's all we'll see, even if it's not really true. We will totally miss the wonderful aspects of life.

Thoughts and attitudes are like colored glass. They accentuate and exaggerate their own colors in the world around us, and they block their opposites from reaching us. (Green leaves through a red lens, for instance, look black.) No matter how grim our present circumstances, an upbeat attitude will, in due time, create upbeat effects. Of that you can be positive.

Keep in Touch

"What do we live for, if not to make things less
difficult for each other?"
—George Eliot

"He climbs highest who helps another up."
—Zig Ziglar

"If I can stop one Heart from breaking
I shall not live in vain
If I can cease one life the aching
Or cool one Pain
Or help one fainting Robin
Unto his Nest again
I shall not live in Vain."
—Emily Dickinson

"Wherever there is a human being, there is an
opportunity for kindness."
—Seneca

When my son was incarcerated in a local jail a few
miles from home, I could see him each Saturday and
Sunday for twenty minutes. Those visits were important to us both but superficial in any kind of personal
sharing, considering the glass partition between us and
the use of phone on either side of the glass. When he
was moved to Texas, he could make occasional phone
calls, but since those too were being monitored, our

conversations were guarded and devoid of any real communication.

Since Rodger has been in Texas, I have been able to make the long trip three times. Realizing that the first trip might be a real challenge in handling feelings, his and mine, I spent time before leaving home and on the plane marshalling my spiritual resources. I was determined that the visit should be a good experience, as pleasant as possible for both of us. I prayed that the people I would meet, the guards, the other families gathered to see their loved ones, the inmates themselves, would receive a blessing of some kind; that peace, harmony, and order would fill the room where we would all gather; that the Spirit of God would be very evident in all the meetings. I asked God to use me as a messenger of His peace and love, wherever and however the message needed to be expressed.

Even before the inmates were brought into the huge, brightly lighted public room, an attractive, elderly black woman came to the little table where I sat waiting for Rodger. She smiled hesitantly, then asked, "Do you believe in prayer?" My heart sang—God had heard my prayer, and I answered, smiling, "Yes, I do. How may I help you?" She sat down quickly and, leaning forward across the table, continued, "Please pray for my son. He's only nineteen and is here because he was caught with a tiny amount of marijuana. He's not a bad boy. He's on the honor roll in his first year of college, and this awful tragedy is ruining his life, and the lives of our whole family. Can God do anything? Do you think He even cares?"

I took her shaking hands in mine and asked God to tell me what to say. I don't remember the words, but I remember the way her tensed, clasped hands began to relax. I assured her that yes, God does care, very much, and that her beloved son is loved by God even more than by her. I got her address and promised to write from time to time, reinforcing the ideas of hope and positive action. I will send her a copy of this book when it is published, along with copies to a number of other mothers I have since met at the prison on my last two visits.

My visits with Rodger were wonderful. We sat across from each other at a small table. Guards wandered about the room but did not intrude on personal conversations. We had no trouble carrying on an animated conversation for the whole four hours, Saturday and Sunday. It was a joy to tell Rodger of all the mail and phone calls expressing love and support for him. I was treated with politeness and consideration by all the guards. One even called a cab for me and let me wait in the front hall, out of the blistering sun.

Our consistent means of communication remains our letters, at least four a week from me, and the same number from Rodger. Before starting a letter, I ask for God's guidance and inspiration for the right words to convey my love and support, praying that the tranquility and confidence I feel might be transmitted to him in spite of the noise, confusion, frustration, and physical discomfort in the beastly hot quarters where there is no relief, day or night. Family news is included, as well as comments on issues he has mentioned in recent letters. Rodger also receives welcome mail from his brother and sister, his sons, our extended family, and many loyal friends. He always responds promptly and gratefully.

I make sure not to add to Rodger's burden with any mention of health problems or other concerns about which he can do nothing. I don't tell him how much I miss his carrying in the groceries, bringing in firewood, or getting me out of a computer crisis. However, I never miss a chance to let him know that he is missed and that there will always be a warm and loving welcome awaiting him. From correspondence with other inmates whom Rodger has befriended, it is clear how much constant reassurance is needed.

When one goes into the prison experience, everything comes to an abrupt halt and the imprisoned person no longer has control over his responsibilities, resulting in unpaid bills, unkept appointments, and unmet commitments at work and home. I can only imagine the panic and feeling of hopelessness that must sweep over one. After the initial shock of Rodger's sudden imprisonment, his sister and I began to face the onslaught of credit card bills, money owed him for rental property, expired licenses. Thanks to Ann's business acumen and her care for her brother's peace of mind, she wrote letters to creditors and got a few adjustments on payments that I could handle, tiny bit by tiny bit. Rodger has expressed his appreciation for this help, and the removal of his concern has been one small way in which we can make this time less stressful for him.

In addition to letters, I send Rodger photocopies of inspirational articles from magazines, once tearing up an entire book of daily readings and sending him ten or twelve pages at a time. I also order at least three books per month to be sent to him from a local bookstore, since the prison does not allow inmates to receive books sent from home. A dear friend also regularly sends books through Amazon.com on a variety of subjects that interest Rodger—science, spirituality, nature, and computer news.

Prison life can be depressing, monotonous, and totally lacking in comfort and familiarity. It is up to us, family and friends, to provide encouragement and support. A letter, a card, a newspaper clipping, or a magazine article can be a crucial link to the outside world for the ones we love.

Rodger speaks:

A person in prison has been stripped of all the major joys in life. Being locked in a cage causes more disruption to one's life than just losing the freedom to move around. Everything that is important has been taken from us and we are left with a few relatively insignificant incidentals. Those little things are then assigned the same importance that used to belong to the big things we no longer possess.

Most of us had lives that were sufficiently busy and full that we weren't concerned whether we received a letter from a loved one. After all, we could always phone them or even visit them. But in prison, where calls and excursions aren't possible, little things like a letter from home take on an enormous emotional significance.

As a person on the inside, I can attest to the importance to my emotional well-being of getting mail from loved ones. In the midst of this darkness, frustration, and hostility, it is easy to forget that we are loved and remembered. I know too many people here who have grown angry and bitter because they have long since stopped receiving mail from home. Letters from loved ones are better than gold—their worth cannot be judged by the relatively small effort required to write them. That simple, caring effort is multiplied many times in importance to those of us who are locked up.

Most prison systems operate commissaries through which inmates can, if they have any money in their commissary account, purchase coffee, snacks, toiletries, and writing materials. Money must be put in their account by someone on the outside. Without money, they are denied even those small pleasures. Being broke and destitute exaggerates the miserable existence that most prisoners must endure. So if you are in a position to contribute a few dollars per week to the account of a loved one in prison, it will be appreciated more than you can imagine. The Center for Positive Living in Ashland sends one hundred dollars per month to my commissary fund to be used entirely to buy treats and a few small "extras" for those who have no such support.

Reach Up, Then Out

"Life's most persistent and urgent question is:
What are you doing for others?"

—Martin Luther King, Jr.

A famous preacher of another era, when asked whether people should see a doctor or simply rely on prayer for healing, answered, "Go first to God, and then to man or woman as God directs."

I agree with that minister's answer. When friends ask how I stay relatively calm and cheerful in the face of Rodger's situation, I reply, "I turn first to God for His peace and comfort and then take whatever further action I am led to take." I have never found that formula to fail.

Emmet Fox, author of many inspiring books, gave a simple suggestion for tackling life's biggest challenges. He called it the Golden Key: "Take your mind off the problem; put your mind on God." Taking your mind off the problem, even for a brief time, refocuses the power of your thought on the positive. Your attention is on God, the good, and infinite possibilities for solutions.

Abraham Lincoln is credited with saying, "A man is what he thinks about all day long." Our problems will stop hanging around when we stop giving them attention.

Will you try spending a few minutes each day thinking about the best outcome for your loved one that you can imagine? Think about how you will feel when your loved one is free. And try looking for the good surrounding you . . . the beauty of nature, the joys of friends, a job well done. When you regularly imagine more good in your life and gratefully acknowledge the good that's already there, more positive events will flow to you and greater peace will fill your being.

After I take the problem to God in prayer, I am often guided to call on professionals, such as other ministers, physicians, and, yes, attorneys for further help. If you feel you would benefit from the help of a professional, ask God or Spirit (or the Force, as my grandson used to label God) for guidance. Then be sure to keep alert for the answer. You may notice an ad in the newspaper or on TV, or you may receive a recommendation from a friend. Perhaps a Web page on the Internet will give you the answer by listing an agency that specializes in the kind of help you need. When you open up to Spirit and simply ask for help, it *will* eventually come—sometimes in the most unexpected ways.

And now comes the reach-out part. When members of my congregation used to phone my office for prayer for a particular problem they faced, we would discuss the situation briefly and I would pray with them on the phone. Then I would ask something of them. Knowing how important it is to take one's mind off the problem, I would give them the names of three people who had also called for prayer. They might know one or more of these three people, but they didn't need to know the problem. (All such matters are confidential when discussed with a minister.) I requested the new caller to reach out, to pray for those three individuals at least twice a day, asking that God's blessings flow into their lives and visualizing them in the light of God's presence. This simple therapy proved to help all concerned. George Gurdjieff, spiritual leader and mystic, tells us, "If you help others, you will be helped, perhaps tomorrow, perhaps in one hundred years, but you will be helped. Nature must pay off the debt. It is a mathematical law, and all life is mathematics."

Sometimes reaching out involves taking action. I never thought of myself as a political activist, but I recently joined a movement of local people determined to abolish the death penalty in this state. My social conscience has become more finely developed as I realize that which hurts another person hurts me and my loved ones. As John Donne poetically put it, "No man is an island. Every man's death diminishes me."

Ethel is a friend who lives in my town and practices many of the ideas I am suggesting. Her daughter has been sentenced to ten years imprisonment in another state for being a murder accomplice, and Ethel is taking care of her daughter's two small children. Ethel lives on a small pension and has some health problems, but she strongly believes she will be able to take care of the children as long as necessary. She also wants to reach out to others who have even fewer resources than she does.

The last time we chatted, Ethel told me she had taken on a new responsibility. She has become a loving foster grandmother to three little girls whose mother has been incarcerated and whose own grandparents have abandoned them. She picks the girls up from school two days a week, brings them to her home for games and snacks, and helps them with homework before returning them to the foster home where they live. She also invites them to spend holidays with her and her grandchildren. Ethel comments, "When I do something kind for someone else, I feel that I am doing it for my daughter. There is little that I can do directly for her these days, but I pray that someone will show her a measure of the kindness that I try to give others."

Can you see, my friend, how your trouble can be the means of opening you up to a more fulfilling life than you have previously known? Like Ethel, we can help and comfort others in ways we never imagined possible. Reach up to God for comfort and reassurance and also to professional helpers, as you are guided. Then reach out to others, passing along to them your newfound faith and confidence in the ultimate good that God has in mind for us all. Some of our greatest blessings come when we're a blessing to others.

Do something for someone else. I know this probably seems like asking too much. Even the simplest gesture of kindness, the most insignificant act of giving on your part, will move you out of your personal grief for a time. Two thoughts cannot occupy the same space at the same time, and when your mind is on helping someone else, it is removed from your own concern. That brief respite is valuable in terms of your own well-being. It gives you a sense of perspective you would otherwise miss.

I believe there is only One life, that life is God, and we are all part of the One life. Therefore, whatever we do for another, we are really doing for everyone, including ourselves. More specifically, it is a cosmic law that what we give out inevitably comes back, some time, in some form. The discovery of this principle is one of the happiest lessons I have learned through this involvement with my son's incarceration.

> May it be, O Lord, that I seek not so much
> to be consoled, as to console
> to be understood, as to understand
> to be loved, as to love.
> For it is in giving oneself that one receives.
> It is in forgetting oneself that one is found.
> It is in pardoning that one obtains pardon.

—St. Francis of Assisi

Rodger adds:

Curiously, it often happens that we receive the most benefit not when we're seeking it for ourselves but rather while providing it to someone else. Perhaps this is because we momentarily forget our own woes while helping others with theirs. It seems that the best way to receive help is to give it, the best way to find a friend is to be one. We never know when something we say in passing will be profoundly meaningful to someone else, making all the difference in how they handle their challenges.

See the Bigger Picture

"The world breaks everyone and afterward
many are strong in the broken places."

—Ernest Hemingway, *A Farewell to Arms*

From the beginning of this puzzling, painful prison episode, a few friends whose insights I admire said, "Try to step back from this immediate 'in your face' condition. Yes, Rodger is in prison. No, there doesn't seem to be any reasonable basis for hope for an early solution. It seems that things are going to continue this way indefinitely. But you've lived long enough to know that there is always more to a situation than meets the eye."

I sensed the truth in these words after a recent visit with Rodger in Texas. I went with the intention of cheering him up, letting him know of all the people who pray for him daily. I found him looking wonderfully calm and strangely at peace, considering the noisy, crowded conditions and the monotony of his days and nights, not to mention the frustration of missing a life of active service in the ministry. To my amazement, I left the prison feeling buoyed up by Rodger's comforting attitude of patience and trust. He is making the best of the trying circumstances and exerting a calming influence on those around him.

Waiting for a cab in a heavy downpour on the second day of my visit, I invited a friendly Hispanic woman to share my umbrella. I had met her on my previous visit. After a thank you, she blurted out, "What in the world is *your* son doing in this place? He *is* your son, right? He looks a little like you." I was tired and not eager to start a long dialogue, so I answered that his "crime" was tossing a little girl in the air and catching her.

She was visibly shocked, as nearly everyone is, upon hearing that explanation. Then, as a dark-haired man in a battered car full of kids pulled up to the curb and honked, she patted my arm and said, "He looks like such a good man . . . maybe God needs him in this miserable place. God bless him." She slid into the front seat of the old car and was gone.

The idea that God needs someone like Rodger, a peacemaker from childhood, in a difficult spot was not new to me. Many friends had suggested the possibility, but I had rejected it as too absurd for consideration. Eventually I began to accept this theory as possible. I believe that the prison experience is part of Rodger's preparation for a larger spiritual work in the future. He is learning important lessons that will be valuable in helping others in similar circumstances. He is exerting a good influence in others' lives. This is verified by letters I've received from inmates who have been with Rodger. One man wrote that Rodger's "patient and caring counseling saved my marriage. I can never thank him enough."

Rodger and I share a basic spiritual tenet that gives meaning to this unwelcome experience: There is only one Life—God, Spirit, Universal Presence, or whatever name we choose to call Divinity. That Life is the primal energy and power in the universe, and each person is a spark or offshoot of that Life force. Each one of us is acting out a role, a part in the earth drama. God—Spirit—wrote the play, directs it, and acts through all of us at all times. When our lives go in unexpected and unwanted directions, we need to accept that as our role for now. The director, God, knows what is necessary for the play's ultimate success.

Perhaps you are thinking, "It's easy for her to find comfort in this matter of taking the long view. Her son is innocent of the charges against him. She has a strong support system of friends and family. She believes in the power of prayer and has a strong faith." You are right, my friend, I am blessed in all these ways, but I have no corner on God's all-encompassing love and mercy. You and your loved one in prison are just as deeply and completely loved as any saint who ever lived.

I'd like to tell you about Tommy, the grandson of a longtime friend. He was raised by Lela, a meek, insecure but well-meaning mother who was married to a bully of a man, Tommy's stepfather. The stepfather regularly beat Lela, sometimes to the point of her needing emergency care. She was so frightened of her husband that she defended him to the authorities and somehow managed to cover up her life of abuse. Tommy, too, was the victim of his stepfather's rage. To protect his mother he also managed to conceal the horrors of his home from the police and social workers.

Hungry for companionship and approval, Tommy connected with a dangerous gang in the sixth grade of his crowded, inner-city school. He began using drugs, stole money, and was arrested at age fourteen and placed in a detention facility. When he came out, he was sent back to his abusive home, where his resolve to go straight was eroded. Another arrest and more prison time followed. Finally, at age nineteen, he was sent to an adult facility where conditions were harsh and frightening.

At this point, Tommy's grandmother, Hannah, wrote to me, asking for help and support. The subject was foreign and forbidding to me at that time. I much preferred to write children's stories, perform weddings, and do other pleasant tasks connected with the ministry. I remember my audacious remark to Hannah during a phone conversation. "You must look away from the pain of the past and of this very moment and take a larger view. What is Tommy learning from this experience? Don't you think he'll profit somehow from this painful time in his life?" I meant well, of course, and was silently asking God to speak through me, but I probably sounded flip and unsympathetic.

I made a few phone calls and found a church in the vicinity of the prison whose minister assured me he would visit Tommy. He added that his church had an active prison ministry. He was as good as his word, for his prayer group and prison ministry team took Tommy under their wing. They visited him regularly and arranged for him to take several classes in practical subjects that would be useful when he was released from prison. Hannah's own church prayer group, my church group, and several other organizations prayed for Tommy daily. We also wrote letters, sent greeting cards on holidays, and had inspirational books sent to him from publishers.

It was a slow process, but today Tommy is gainfully employed in a trade he learned in prison. He lives with his mother, who finally had the courage to leave her abusive husband. Tommy and his mother have become active members of the church that gave him so much help during his imprisonment. His grandmother, Hannah, now spends much of her retirement leisure writing to some of Tommy's fellow inmates who are still incarcerated. She has even "adopted" a young woman in one of the facilities not far from her home. Tommy drives his grandma to the prison every Sunday to visit this girl and, according to the observant grandma, there seems to be a growing attraction between the two young people. Who but God knows what the larger picture will reveal in the future?

If we could only see the overall plan for our lives, we would know that plan includes joy and sorrow, comfort and pain. These painful times come to us for our growth and maturity. Although we resist them, they are a natural part of God's plan. I recall telling my congregation that life is like a mosaic—the dark pieces are as necessary as the bright ones in the overall perfection of the piece of art. Although we'd prefer to have only light, bright, happy experiences, how can we truly appreciate the bright times if we don't have the contrasts of the dark ones?

I lovingly invite you to consider the larger picture in your life and that of your loved one. God makes no mistakes but uses all of ours for good, in some inexplicable divine way. Sometimes a bone is stronger after having been broken and then healed. For many years I suffered pain and discomfort from an old disease that eventually left me unable to walk. After a complete knee replacement surgery a year ago, I am experiencing pain-free walking. With the help of calcium supplementation, exercise, and powerful affirmations of wholeness, the bones in that leg are stronger than ever.

I've shared previously how a miracle happened when I was a young woman. My right leg was an inch shorter than the other, the result of that same childhood illness. After I married and had a child, my right leg began to grow—imperceptibly at first and then more noticeably. In less than a year, my leg grew to just the right length and I could wear two identical shoes instead of one with an inch-high lift in it. Years later, I was minister of a church in Arcadia, California, and director of the Barnhart School, connected with the church. Each morning, I conducted chapel services in the sanctuary for the children and faculty and I would tell the new students about my marvelous healing. One day I had finished telling them that the divine intelligence in my body knew just how long to grow that leg, and a small girl on the front row raised her hand. With wide eyes she exclaimed, "Wow, Dr. Stevens! Aren't you glad that it stopped growing when it did?"

My friend, that Power, Energy, and Intelligence that knew how long to grow my leg knows exactly what is best for you and your loved ones. If given the chance, it will bring into your life the very conditions, events, and circumstances that will allow you to be all you were created to be—a happy, fulfilled, contributing member of the human race.

Rodger says:

As we have already noted, the prison experience is not strictly limited to the one who has been incarcerated but includes those who remain on the outside to carry on their lives as best they can. When disaster strikes—and the prison experience is definitely a disaster—we seek to find under-standing and perspective as to why this has hap-pened.

The temptation is to look no further than the cir-cumstances themselves, as though the reasons things happened to us are somehow independent of the rest of the universe, as though our lives and our being are not really connected to everything else. When we look no further, we limit our understanding to what might be called "the small-er picture." The smaller picture consists of what we think we know about life, who we are, how things work, where things fit, and so on. We become complacent when we look no further . . . we think we already know, so why ask ques-tions? The smaller picture is the world known through our senses.

Jarring experiences have a way of rousing us from our slumber, waking us to the fact that our smaller picture is woefully incomplete and inac-curate. We know what we know, but we don't know what we don't know. Ironically, when we begin to understand the extent of the things we don't know, we begin to realize how little we real-ly understand the things we thought we already knew!

The larger picture extends far beyond the quaint borders of our personal smaller pictures. It is the vast preponderance of reality, both intimately near and cosmically distant, that is unavailable to our senses. "What it is" is therefore largely a mat-ter of speculation, a collection of deductions based on such tenuous standards as philosophical axioms and religious dogma. It is ultimately per-sonal in that each one of us has a different under-standing of it. The absolute can never be known through relativistic tools like the human intellect and its arsenal of physical senses, hence humankind's history of disagreement and subsequent bloodshed and suffering when this is forgotten.

What is the larger picture? Why have these disasters chosen to impose themselves in our lives? I can only offer my own understanding in answer to such a question. At best, my understanding might serve as a useful metaphor, but statements of absolute truth are impossible using any symbolic language. Or, as Lao-tzu put it, "The truth which can be spoken or written is not the true truth." Religion is a metaphor. Even language is a metaphor. Once this is clearly grasped, we begin to migrate from our smaller picture to a larger one that affirms far more of our divinity than was possible before. This is how it looks to me. . . .

Humanity is on the cusp of a new age. The social arrangements that have dominated the past few thousand years of human life have reached the limits of their usefulness and spilled over into years of diminishing returns. This human experience is readying itself to move upward once again, leaving behind the base and raw instinctual motivations that have colored these early states—greed, isolation, competition, fear, control, and all manifestations of an ego that has fallen out of touch with its own deeper realities.

Each of us, regardless of our earthly situations, is here to learn those things that can only be communicated through our present circumstances. Each of us is being readied and prepared to move into new dimensions of existence. They will be so different that their descriptions probably wouldn't make any sense to us now.

We needn't be concerned. We need only trust that Life knows what it's about, that it is our nature to flow toward our greater good. Human institutions based on fear, coercion, guilt, anger, and retribution have almost run their course, and we are experiencing their dying days.

The details of our personal lives are no more significant to our cosmic well-being than, say, the details of a movie script to the real life of the actor portraying a part in that movie. It all seems quite real until we wake up and realize that it isn't real—it's just a movie, a dance of light on the screen.

As we seek to find out who we really are, we find that we can never become a known definition, for we are infinite. We can use all our present circumstances and experiences as proof that there is infinitely more to us than meets the eye. We can live with forgiveness and trust. We can surrender to the higher truths of our being, which is already perfect. We can learn to guard our consciousness against negative thoughts as the lions guard the door to the temple.

We are right where we need to be to take the shortest route to happiness and fulfillment. Let's be where we are . . . accept our divinity. That's all.

The Amazing Results of Surrender

"Let go and let God."

It has become increasingly obvious to me that every situation in life—the welcome and pleasant, the difficult and dreaded—is significant for one reason: We have a lesson to learn, something we need to experience if we are to fulfill our purpose for being on Earth at this time.

Since my son's prison life began, I have pursued many possible paths that might lead to his freedom. Those wiser than I, watching my sometimes frantic efforts to change Rodger's situation, have gently suggested that it was time to surrender the results to a Higher Power. I have sometimes equated that step as giving up, or giving in to what seems like the inevitable supremacy of the prison system (still one of my biggest challenges in the forgiveness department!).

For years I prattled on about "Let go and let God" with little deep thought about what it really means. Does it mean to just sit back and let life happen to us?

I don't think so. There are some biblical references on the subject of surrender. One of my favorites is, "Having done all, stand." To me, this phrase means that after we have done everything humanly possible, we can leave the results to God.

Some weeks ago, I happened on a televised Sunday morning worship service from a large church in Atlanta. I was delighted to find that the guest speaker was Dr. Lloyd Ogilvie, a remarkably effective and moving speaker to whom I often listened when he was pastor of the huge Hollywood Presbyterian Church in California. For many years, Dr. Ogilvie has been the chaplain of the U.S. Senate, and in his TV sermon he spoke of weekly prayer breakfasts attended by many members of the Senate. (I was glad to hear that *some* of our politicians still believe in prayer!) He shared an eight-word slogan that they used as a sort of cornerstone of the prayer breakfast discussions: "Without God, we can't. Without us, God won't." Think about that statement for a moment. Can you believe that God needs you to bring order and resolution to the stormy places in your life or in the lives of those you love? But you can't do this alone, only as God works in and through you. It's a partnership, with God bearing the ultimate responsibility for the way things turn out.

Essential to the letting go is the absolute and unshakable belief that God loves us beyond description and forever wants the highest and best of everything for us. Letting go does not mean abandoning our hopes and dreams to a mysterious force that may or may not see fit to answer our prayers. It means giving up the lesser for the greater result. Another comforting bit of scripture comes to mind: "Stand still and see the salvation of the Lord." That means stop frantically running around, desperately searching for answers. Stop all effort for a while and take time to visualize the end result, the perfect answer to the problem.

Instead of seeing surrender as I used to see it, with fear and insecurity, I now know that surrender means turning the matter over to the indwelling Christ, the very presence of God within me. I know that no other being, human or divine, cares so deeply for me and for those I love. And no other power can bring about beneficial changes that can surpass my highest hopes.

Robin is a friend who has been envied by those who know her. Her life was filled with what many people desire—a great husband, three bright children, a gorgeous home on the oceanfront, a successful writing career, physical beauty, and radiant good health. She had it all. Then Robin's world began to unravel. Her marriage became troubled, her sixteen-year-old daughter got pregnant and dropped out of high school, her next two books weren't successful, and her publisher dropped her. To top it off, she was diagnosed with breast cancer.

Robin followed all the techniques and exercises she had written about in her self-help books. She fanatically set about fixing all the problems in her life. One day, in a tearful confession to an old college friend who had become a minister, she said, "I'm so tired. I just want to die and get out of this mess for good. I've done everything I know to do and nothing works . . . I give up."

Her friend John took Robin's cold hand in his and said, "Finally. Now God has a chance." He then prayed a simple prayer of release and surrender, giving control of Robin's life to her own indwelling Christ who loved her with an all-encompassing compassion.

Several years later as she told me of that life-changing afternoon, Robin explained that as John prayed for her, a great weight seemed to fall from her heart. She suddenly felt lighter and more vibrant than she had in years. John gave her several suggestions on how to keep on "letting go" at times when she felt the old tension and anxiety returning.

Change came gradually. Robin's first decision after the visit with John was to declare a year of inactivity in her writing career and to spend more time working on the restoration of her marriage. Her husband responded to her decision with renewed dedication to their relationship. As their home became more peaceful and harmonious, problems with their pregnant daughter began to smooth out. The girl returned to school and during the summer gave birth to a beautiful baby, whom her parents adopted. With her job stress removed for awhile, Robin recovered quickly and completely from cancer surgery. She eventually returned to her career with new insights and a much broader field of experience to share with future readers.

Robin fairly glowed as she filled me in on the particulars of her new life. "The bottom line, Margaret," she said with a smile, "is that now I know God's will is always for good, and greater good than I could ever dream up."

When I was a little girl, I carefully kept my mouth shut or, afraid of being discovered as a blasphemer, simply mouthed the words to "Thy will be done" in the Lord's prayer at church. When our Sunday school class worked on a project to help missionaries in South Africa, I was deathly afraid that if I prayed, "Thy will be done," God would ship me off to that miserable land of wild animals, cannibals, and awful heat.

Many years later, I stepped off a plane at the huge Jan Smuts Airport in Johannesburg, South Africa, and was greeted by a welcoming group of loving people—black, white, and those of mixed parentage. I instantly fell in love with the country and the people. Over the next twenty years, I enjoyed six more wonderful visits to that beautiful land. Each time I thanked God that I had finally decided to pray the Lord's Prayer properly, with special emphasis on "Thy will be done."

That short phrase is even more meaningful to me these days. Although I want my son safely home, free to live his life to the fullest, I have come to the realization that God's will for Rodger has more treasures and blessings than I could ever imagine (and my imagination can get pretty wild!). I do not have the right to choose Rodger's path based on my limited thinking and understanding, but I do have the right and responsibility to pray for God's will to be done in his life. I know that God's will is always for the greater good and affects many people and circumstances, not just His plans for my son alone. I end each day by sending Rodger deep love and blessings, thanking God and the angels for loving and protecting him. I ask them to let him know how much he is loved and supported by so many. And I always close my prayer with "Thy will be done." Then I go to sleep, feeling that I have given Rodger the best possible gift, knowing that God is working all things together for good for us all because we put His will first in our lives.

Remember, my friend, as you surrender to the Divine, you are exchanging your limited, human concept of good for an infinitely greater expression of good, not only for your loved ones but for the many whose lives they will touch. God will honor your surrender of the little dream for the greater one, and you will be able to pray "Thy will be done" with a new sense of meaning and freedom. God bless you!

Rodger comments:

I resisted the idea of surrender when it was first proposed to me. Here in the Western world, it is considered an indication of weakness or lack of resolve to give in, to quit fighting before victory is attained. To yield the field supposedly proves a lack of character. It's entirely an ego thing.

Ego is, of course, the whole problem. We weren't born with an ego—it was acquired. Ego is the composite self-image that we built up, especially in childhood, from bits and pieces of everything everyone has ever told us about ourselves. Our ego was formed as parents praised or ridiculed us, as peers embraced or shunned us, as teachers and other authority figures rewarded or punished us. We were left with the net impression of "who the world thinks we are." Since part of our socialization process consisted in eroding our belief in our own sovereignty and validity, we came to accept society's verdict of who we are.

Our egos are generally fragile and easily damaged. As long as we are convinced that these fragile constructs are who we are, then we will struggle to protect them with our very lives, if necessary. We are delighted when others approve of us and devastated when they disapprove of us because we are "hooked" on approval. Consequently, the idea of surrendering—to God, to fate, to the inevitable—feels suicidal to the timorous, quaking ego.

Surprisingly it is this very surrender that reveals to us who we really are. We are like actors in a play who have forgotten that it is only a play and our egos are only the roles we assume. We've been brainwashed into believing that the roles are who we really are. Because these roles, these egos, feel so vulnerable, we desperately try to control the action on the stage. But the ego has no idea what the play is about or what is the intent of the playwright (God). If that role or ego begins to act out of character—trying to be someone he is not, even though society may push him to do just that—then he will disrupt the flow of the play for others. When such "lost roles" constitute the vast majority of humankind, as is the case today, then the violence and unhappiness we see around us makes sense.

When we surrender, we don't just go "Poof!" in a cloud of purple smoke. We are still actors playing the roles that are called by our names. But for perhaps the first time since childhood, we will sense that we are not that role but the actor playing the role. The difference is enormous, because when we surrender to Life, to God, to Jesus, or to Buddha (to whom or what we surrender doesn't really matter), then we begin to return to being in tune with reality.

We are part of Life—call it God if you wish—and Life is part of us. Life wants us to be happy, so it sends us experiences intended and designed to get us back on the right track, in tune with reality. Life won't be as happy as it can be until we are happy, and we won't be happy until we give up trying to control things but rather relax into that effortless state of being who we really are.

Life knows far better than we possibly could what needs to happen and when. The sooner we can "get out of the way" (both God's and our own), the sooner we can devote that now-wasted energy to purposes that really do make life better for everyone.

I am using this time in prison to work on myself, to surrender egocentric attitudes and tendencies that I've accumulated over the course of my life. I'm learning the difference between who I've been told I am and who I really am, the difference between the roles I'm playing and the actor who's playing the roles. That actor existed before the role was created and will continue to exist after I turn this disguise back to the property room when my final curtain descends.

I am learning to surrender and allow Life to place me where it wants me, for I know that therein lies my greatest meaning and fulfillment.

Trust, Trust, Then Trust
Some More

*"If the Bible could be summed up in two words,
they would be, 'Trust Me.'"*

—Tim Reins

Much of our life is built on simple trust. We trust that the sun will come up tomorrow. Even though clouds may obscure the sky, we know that the sun is behind the clouds in its usual place, ready to appear in all its glory when the clouds move away. We trust that the food we buy and eat is pure and nourishing, that the chair on which we sit will hold us up. In recent years, our blind trust in certain areas of the government, the justice system, and some of our politicians has eroded and we have become unwilling to trust as implicitly as we did in the past.

That growing fear and lack of faith in many of the institutions of our past can make us a little nervous about surrendering our goals, our hopes, and dreams to a force or power as nebulous and unknown as God. The answer to that reluctance is to learn more about the Supreme Being, the one to whom we can entrust our most cherished dreams.

History is rich in stories on this very theme. My favorite is the Old Testament story of Job, a man who knew God as few did in that age of superstition and uncertainty. Through all the traumatic experiences of his life, Job communicated with God and loved and served God to the best of his ability.

Now, Job was a very fortunate man. He owned great wealth in herds of animals, fertile crops, and other forms of earthly riches. He was blessed with a loving wife (although, when the chips were down, she was not a supportive mate). They had seven sons and three daughters.

According to the Bible narrative, at the high point in Job's life the devil entered the picture. (The devil was the embodiment and personification of evil in that ancient culture.) The devil set about wooing Job from his allegiance to God, and he spared no mercy. Suddenly Job's crops were destroyed. Then his herds were stolen or slaughtered. His children died in the collapse of a building destroyed in a strong wind. Job's wife urged him to just curse God and die. Yet he refused to give up his trust in God. He responded, "We have been blessed with God's blessings. Shall we not also receive His afflictions?" (In Old Testament days, people understood God as a tyrannical Being, capable of great wrath and destruction.)

Although Job was steadfast, he continued to suffer in all possible ways, including suffering from painful boils that covered his body. He never gave up his absolute faith in God's goodness. Many chapters later in the story, we learn that everything that was taken from Job was restored, with even more than he originally possessed. He had greater material wealth, more children (same old wife, it seems), and good health in his later years. Job's immortal statement has stood through the centuries as an inspiration to those of us who tend to doubt and question God's wisdom and guidance: "Though he slay me, yet will I trust Him." So, my friend, when you find yourself ready to give up, to lose faith, remember Job, and rejoice if someone says to you, "You have the patience of Job."

I can recall many instances when I chose to trust God's plan instead of wallowing in discouragement, using only my limited, human thinking. Each time my trust was justified. I could write a book about solutions that came at the last minute, in a perfect manner, just when there seemed no possible way out.

Late one night I was stranded in the San Francisco airport because I had missed the last connecting flight home to Oregon. I stood in a long line waiting for help at the customer service counter. My knee hurt from having run to try to catch the departing plane, carrying a heavy carry-on bag, and wearing a winter coat. Exhausted, I just wanted to sit down and have a good cry. Then I remembered Emerson's magnificent statement that has helped me many times: "The things I have seen teach me to trust the Creator for the things that I have not seen." I recalled other times of crisis, similar circumstances, and that lost, lonely, panicky feeling. I silently repeated one of the most effective prayers I've ever found: "Father, I'm trusting." I silently repeated the words until I reached the counter where a customer service representative was wearily asking, "How may I help you?" Someone had left a small bag in front of the counter and, in my haste, I tripped over it and started to fall. Suddenly two strong arms caught me and I looked up into the kindly face of a gray-haired "angel."

I thanked the man, but he didn't leave. He stood

there as I talked with the agent, who gave me a voucher for a hotel for the night and arranged a reservation on the first morning plane to Medford. The waiting man picked up my bag and led me out of the crowd to a bench where a sweet-faced, middle-aged woman waited. He introduced her as his wife and, turning to me, said, "I didn't mean to eavesdrop, but I know it's no fun to be stranded in a strange city at this time of night. Our limousine is waiting just outside, and my wife and I would like to take you to your hotel. It's in a rather seamy part of town." My first impulse was to refuse the offer as my mother's warning about accepting favors from strangers arose from the past. But I remembered that I had prayed for help and must trust that the right kind of help would appear.

So, still trusting that I was doing the right thing, I rode to the hotel in luxury with my new friends. The man gave me his business card. He was the CEO of a huge banking concern in San Francisco, and their address was an impressive one. Arriving at the hotel, he insisted that I stay in the warm car with his wife while he checked me in. Then he came and got me, carried my bag to the elevator, tipped his hat as my father always did so gallantly, and said goodnight. The bellboy who took me to my room remarked, "That man must be a good friend—he spent more than five minutes at the check-in desk making sure that you have a nice room and that you will have breakfast served in your room." Then, smiling broadly, he added, "He even gave me the biggest tip I've had in days—nice guy." I echoed those words, nice guy, and silently thanked God. I've found that when God honors our trust, He does it first-class.

In this process of trying to help my son, I have

done everything I know to do. I have followed every lead. I have written letters to people I thought might be helpful. I have enlisted the help of many friends in a letter-writing campaign to the parole board. I have given Rodger's name to countless prayer groups throughout the country and in other parts of the world. Now it is time to say, with Job, "I will continue to trust God, no matter what." He loves me. He loves my son more than I could possibly love him. He is using Rodger to help other inmates in ways that only Rodger can do. Certainly I don't like waiting for him to come home. I dread thinking about him day after day, night after night, in that depressing, confining prison, but God must have some very good and important reason for this situation. Once again, the things that I have seen teach me to trust the Creator for the things I have not seen.

A few years ago in a message that Rodger gave at our Center for Positive Living here in Ashland, he used this traffic illustration. You are driving along, making good time on your trip, and suddenly there is an abrupt halt. Traffic stands still, horns start honking, people shout to other motorists. A few people get out of their cars to peer down the road ahead but can't see anything that explains the tie-up. Up above there is a helicopter hovering over the scene. The pilot sees an accident on the highway some distance ahead. Over his loudspeaker, he bellows out orders for a slight detour until the accident is cleared away. Drivers get in their cars, follow orders, and soon are on their way again with little time lost.

God is the celestial helicopter pilot who sees all the aspects of every situation. He knows the solutions and gives the best directions for all concerned. If we choose to ignore His guidance, we could become embroiled indefinitely in a traffic jam. But as we look to him, He will get us on the road again.

Tension and worry are gradually leaving my heart and mind. Sleep is easier and more restful now that I am releasing Rodger's situation every night and every morning to God's loving care. The Bible tells us to "cast your burdens on the Lord," and that is what trusting is all about. My friend, I urge you to follow, as completely as you can, the simple steps you have found in this little book. I promise you that when you get to the point of deeply trusting, you will find a peace and comfort you may never have experienced in your life. God bless you!

> I will not worry, fret, or be unhappy over you.
> I will not be anxious concerning you.
> I will not be afraid for you.
> I will not blame you, criticize, or condemn you.
> I will remember first, last, and always that you
> are God's child,
> That you have His Spirit in you.
> I will trust this Spirit to take care of you, to be
> a light to your path,
> to provide for your needs.
> I will think of you always as being surrounded
> by God's care, as being
> kept safe and secure in Him.
> I will be patient with you.
> I will have confidence in you.
> I will stand by in faith and bless you in my
> prayers, knowing that you
> are finding the help you need.
> I have only good feelings in my heart about
> you, for I am willing to let
> you live your life as you see fit.

Your way may not be my way, but I will trust
the Spirit of God to show
you the way of your highest good.

—Anonymous

Rodger comments:

Trust is the twin of surrender. They serve together. Surrender occurs when we realize that our
ego is an illusion and we relinquish our belief in
its reality. Trust is the sense that beneath all the
emotion and sensations of life, "who we really
are" was never and can never be in jeopardy.
Trust, like surrender, is letting go of the urge to
control the results of our efforts or to control other
people and events in ways that we think are best.
Trust occurs when we are in an airplane in chop-
py air, having confidence in the pilot and fully
knowing that we couldn't do the job ourselves.
Trust is letting go.
If we believe in God's omniscience, omnipo-
tence, and omnipresence, then trust is simply
acknowledging that God knows what is happening and what is supposed to happen. Nothing
ever happens without God's permission, knowledge, and complete involvement, even events
that we might term the very worst—and for
which we try to assign human blame, guilt, and
retribution. Even the worst we could imagine
couldn't happen without God's agreement,
though God's purposes and motives remain safely beyond our grasp. Trust is the acknowledg-
ment that if it happens, then it is somehow all
right. As the saying goes, "Things are always
okay, even when they're not."
Trust is accepting that when the time is right, all
this craziness will make some kind of sense to us.

In the meantime, our lack of understanding is okay, too. We can't be expected to know what hasn't been made available to us yet. As stated before, we know what we think we know, but we don't know what we don't know. Trust is the acceptance that it's all somehow okay.

What the Attitude of Gratitude Can Do for You

"Praise God even when you don't understand
what He is doing."
—Henry Jacobsen

Developing an attitude of gratitude may be the most significant step you can take to restore peace of mind and a positive approach to your challenges. When I review what I have learned through my son's prison experience, I can honestly say that becoming more aware of my blessings and giving continual thanks has brought the greatest help and comfort of any practice I've found. I have learned that some of the greatest blessings come disguised as problems, and I'm learning to give thanks even for them!

It's easy to give thanks for the good things that come into our lives. But giving thanks for *everything*, as Paul instructs in the Bible? Even the broken leg, the tax audit, the *imprisonment*? Yes, the act of being thankful for our problems seems to be the magic key to the fulfillment of our deepest desires. It is, of course, much easier to complain, to feel sorry for ourselves, to accept a victim role. But that path leads nowhere but to more problems.

Catherine Ponder, in her excellent book *The Dynamic Laws of Healing* (1966) writes:

> Many physical ills and certainly most mental ills are due, consciously or unconsciously, to feelings of resentment. *You cannot be grateful and resentful at the same time.* When you feel a surge of resentment, because of some slight, hurt, or disappointment, deliberately change the direction of your feelings by thinking of something for which you are grateful.
>
> Make a practice of praising your problems, troubles, and difficult experiences. As you do, you will find that you can be grateful for the experience that previously made you resentful, since that resentment finally caused you to cultivate the praiseful, thankful state of mind. Any experience that leads you to a deeper degree of good should be praised. Every sorrow, disappointment, and hard experience is trying to lead you to greater understanding, which, in turn, leads to a better way of life. Therefore, your hard experiences should be praised. They are a blessing in disguise. According to a fifteenth-century mystic, there is a radiance, a shining forth in our dark experiences, could we but see it.

Catherine Ponder shares the experience of one of her readers, a homemaker who was experimenting with these powerful principles. The woman wrote, "I have learned that I can always resort to the act of thanksgiving with good results. No matter what the situation, the words, 'Thank you, God,' open the way for better living. Health, prosperity, and peace come when one begins thanking God in the midst of dark experiences."

When we can accept the premise that there are no accidents or coincidences, only connections we cannot see, when we give up our victim role and see ourselves as cocreators of great good for ourselves and our loved ones, then we can know that wonderful, almost unbelievable, surprises are awaiting us.

The subject of gratitude and appreciation has had worldwide attention recently, largely through the television programs hosted by Oprah Winfrey. Years ago this successful public figure began to promote the idea of keeping a gratitude journal. I joined the millions who bought notebooks and began this simple but amazingly powerful way of increasing the quantity and quality of blessings in our lives. For four years I have continued this nightly practice of writing down at least six things—events, conditions, material items—for which I'm grateful. I now have eight notebooks full of expressions of gratitude. Some nights I use an entire page. Looking back through those notebooks is the most uplifting, therapeutic spirit-raiser I have found.

You may be asking the same question I asked in the beginning of my adventure in gratitude: "How can I thank God for the miserable life my loved one will be enduring for who-knows-how-long? What can I possibly find for which to be thankful in this awful situation?" I know just how you feel, my friend. I've been there. I found my way out of that defeated, hopeless well of depression when I reasoned this way:

If I believe that all things work together for good to those who love God and put Him first in their lives . . . *if* I accept the truth that there are no accidents or events without purpose and meaning . . . *if* I trust that God's plan for my dear one's life is far greater than anything I could dream up, and . . . *if* I am willing to move beyond the pain and uncertainty of this experience, to the perfect outcome for all concerned—God's plan, brought about in God's perfect time and God's perfect way . . . *then*, and only *then*, can I wholeheartedly thank God for this situation. As I put all my love and attention on the perfect outcome, as I praise and thank God for His promise to "deliver us from evil," then I can rest in the security of His love and provision in all aspects of my life and the life of my loved one.

Many nights I have prayed, "Thank you, God, that my son is where he is. Thank you for using his light, his awareness of his Oneness with God, in a place of pain and darkness. Thank you for your constant love and protection surrounding and infilling him, right where he is. I praise you and thank you for your perfect plan for his life, which is unfolding day by day, no matter what appearances to the contrary may be. Thank you, thank you, thank you!" Then I spend a few quiet minutes resting in the peaceful place within, where I feel God's presence so strongly. I know, with a deep inner knowing that nothing can shake, God is in charge and my gratitude and appreciation of that truth is hastening the day when my son will step out of prison life, free at last to share the insights and lessons he has learned in this "graduate school" of earth experience.

Our thoughts and words create our reality. As we begin to praise and thank God for everything in our lives, the answers we seek begin to materialize. The added bonus of a peace that passes all understanding will be with us always, in all circumstances.

Strange as it seems, even to me, I find myself giving thanks daily, almost hourly, for these past eight years. I have learned much about myself, why I am here, and how my life can be meaningful in the remaining years on Earth. I have discovered that age has nothing to do with our potential for serving, being of value to others, and making our own unique contribution to our world. I have found a new richness, a new beauty in the most commonplace situations and events. To my great joy and delight, I have found greater faith in the eternal goodness of God, in the depth of His love and compassion, and in a bright future for all people who awaken to the truth of their own being.

My friend, I have no idea of the degree to which your life may be in turmoil at this very moment, but I assume that you are reading this book because you want and need help in crisis or challenge. I pray that the words you have read—straight from my heart and Rodger's heart—may inspire, encourage, and support you in your journey from fear to faith.

God bless you!

Any moment of hating
  Any moment of lying,
    Any moment of resentment,
      Is a moment of dying.

      Any moment of loving,
        Any moment of giving,
          Any moment of thankfulness,
            Is a moment of living.

—Anonymous

Some Closing Thoughts
from Rodger

It would probably be appropriate to say more about how I feel about my imprisonment, though I must immediately add that one cannot rise above the pain while reminiscing, weighed down by the emotional burdens that readily arise under these circumstances.

I have perhaps run the gamut of negative emotions since this ordeal began. Guilt or innocence has next to nothing to do with how we humans respond to the loss of our freedom and liberties, for there is something deep within each of us that resents the imposition of hardship and extreme limitations. This resentment is only heightened when one realizes that those responsible for enforcing our so-called justice system are no different from those upon whom it is imposed, that the "innocent-until-proven-guilty" standard is a fairy tale, or that fairness, balance, and perspective are not part of the foundations of modern justice.

Only a saint can remain emotionally neutral when his reputation is unilaterally trashed, when exaggerations against him attain the status of fact, when one side of a dispute is considered to be the only side, when his career, his possessions, his savings, his reputation—everything he has worked for—are incidentally swept away because he has been denied the right to preserve them. Only a saint.

But I am not a saint. Like you, I am still trying to dig my way out from under the lies and disinformation I was fed in school, in church, and through the media, still dealing with the frustration and anger that arises when I realize how I was misled, and the degree to which I was misled. Prisons are an abominable waste of human life and resources. They are the most striking evidence of the failure of the culture that maintains and supports them.

But saying so doesn't improve my position. Being righteously outraged won't set me free, and it won't prevent countless others from falling prey to this same fate. When I think about my anger and frustration, I run a risk, because there are no pressure valves here, no vents for the intense pressures that are the rule when unfairness prevails. Without a tree to kick or a rock to break, the raw emotions spawned by these pressures turn and eat us from within. Not healthy in the least.

So during the time I have been locked up, I have been working on myself, looking for ways to get past these hurtful and unhealthy emotions, looking deep within myself for the truths that I've failed to find out there in the world of laws, religion, and philosophy. If I am in this situation, then regardless of the so-called causes for my being here, this must necessarily be where what we call God wants me to be. If I would do justice to that, then my habits and desire to be emotionally incensed, my rage, my anger, and frustration and regrets and shame and remorse, all these must be swept away.

Easier said than done, of course. But it is the purpose of books like this to let it be known that there are alternative ways of living with imprisonment, ways that are not filled with black rage and red-hot anger but, rather, ways that use these circumstances to move beyond, for the caterpillar of our old selves to use this cocoon of prison to become the butterflies we are all destined to be. If my contributions to this book seem too cerebral, too devoid of emotion, it is because I am still a work in progress. I am still looking for what works. But I think I have found, for myself, anyway, that emotions are not the answer, that at best they can lead us to deeper aspects of our being, but only if we recognize them to be symptomatic of deeper perceptions.

There are countless books available today on the search for Truth. Some are better than others. But the searcher will always be provided with the next place to put his foot, the next handhold in his climb to the light. If you honestly want to know the truth, then you are already on the path to finding it, and though it sometimes seems incredible, the circumstances in which you find yourself are absolutely the best possible; if some other setting were better, God would have put you there instead.

In the meantime, love yourself, even if it seems that nobody else does, for who you are is infinite, timeless, and perfect. Be who you already are.

Epilogue

There is always a sequel to the kind of story you have just read. In this case, it is not what I would like to report—that my son has been pardoned and is happily getting on with a full and productive life among family and friends. No, he is still incarcerated in a Texas prison, with a full year to serve before being eligible for parole. All efforts at obtaining his release have proved futile. There have been many dead ends in following leads, looking into agencies that might help, hopefully searching for the answer to a speedy end to this nightmare.

So what is there to write about as an epilogue? It is simply that the real significance of this painful episode in our lives is beginning to appear, slowly but surely. Many friends have become aware of the injustice, debasement, and inhumanity of the present justice system and are making their voices heard in local and statewide protests for change. I am constantly amazed at the number of close friends who have become involved in some form of activity in prison reform because of Rodger's situation. One longtime friend has become interested in the rehabilitation programs in both Texas and Oregon and is leaning toward an active political career. He and his wife are committed to giving their time, energy, and considerable knowledge and social connections to some kind of reform in the prison scene.

Personally, this experience has opened me to a world of possibilities for spending the remaining years of my life in service to hurting families. Our family has come even closer together in efforts to support and encourage Rodger and keep the lifeline of love for each other strong and invincible. My constant prayer these past seven years has been for God to use this greatest of all tests as a blessing for others. That prayer is being answered daily.

When Rodger and I embarked on the project of this book, I had hoped, as had others, that he would write more about his personal challenges in prison—his feelings of victimhood, anger, frustration, and the bitter disappointment in losing so many valuable years of a worthwhile life to a totally undeserved exile. I am coming to understand the problems of sharing those emotions and reactions from the confinement of prison, the crowded, noisy dorm with sixty-five angry men in one space, the lack of privacy and silence, the horrid heat and humidity during the summer months, and the boredom of daily routine. With all mail, incoming and outgoing, opened and read by examiners, the possibility of getting the real feel of the place out into the world is relatively small, if even possible.

Rodger wrote the short essays in this book to help the families of prisoners. No doubt when he is free and back at his beloved computer, the full story of his experience will be forthcoming. Until then, this will suffice, we hope.

One of my goals is to establish our web page to be able to answer mail on the Internet and minister to people in a very real and personal way, and to share information about possible resources and agencies that can assist with legal procedures. This must wait until Rodger is home to help me, but it will be done.

In the meantime, thank you for reading our story and know that we want to help *you* find the acceptance, peace of mind, and trust in your own life purpose. God bless you always and in all ways.

Literature Cited

Benson, Herbert. 1975. *The Relaxation Response.* New York: Morrow.

Caddy, Eileen. 1996. *Opening Doors Within.* N.p.: Findhorn Press.

Ferrini, Paul. 1991. *The Twelve Steps of Forgiveness.* Brattleboro, Vt.: Heartways Press.

Gibran, Kahlil. 1946. *The Prophet.* New York: Knopf.

Jampolsky, Gerald G. 1999. *Forgiveness: The Greatest Healer of All.* Hillsboro, Or.: Beyond Words Publishing, Inc.

———. 1979. *Love Is Letting Go of Fear.* Millbrae, Calif.: Celestial Arts.

Peale, Norman Vincent. 1952. *The Power of Positive Thinking.* New York: Prentice-Hall.

Ponder, Catherine. 1966. *The Dynamic Laws of Healing.* West Nyack, N.Y.: Parker Publishing Company.

Walsch, Neale Donald. 1996. *Conversations with God: An Uncommon Dialogue, Book 1.* New York: G. P. Putnam's Sons.

———.1997. *Conversations with God: An Uncommon Dialogue, Book 2.* Charlottesville, VA: Hampton Roads Publishing Co., Inc.

———.1998. *Conversations with God: An Uncommon Dialogue, Book 3.* Charlottesville, VA: Hampton Roads Publishing Co., Inc.

———.1996. *Friendship with God: An Uncommon Dialogue.* New York: Putnam.

White Eagle. 1972. *The Quiet Mind.* N.p.: White Eagle Publishing Trust

About the Authors

Kathy Hollis Cooper, 2001

Kathy Hollis Cooper, 2001

Margaret and Rodger Stevens are a mother and son who are both ordained ministers in the "New Thought": metaphysically oriented spiritual doctrines that are the foundation of such churches as Unity and Religious science. In 1993, Rodger was accused of a crime and later sentenced to eight years in a Texas prison. Margaret and Rodger state this was a false accusation, and have found the experience to be a grueling test of their faith in God and their ability to love unconditionally. They put their experiences, and the lessons they learned, in writing to be an inspiration for others who find themselves in similar circumstances. Margaret lives in Ashland, Oregon.

WALSCH BOOKS is an imprint of Hampton Roads Publishing Company, edited by Neale Donald Walsch and Nancy Fleming-Walsch. Our shared vision is to publish quality books that enhance and further the central messages of the *Conversations with God* series, in both fiction and non-fiction genres, and to provide another avenue through which the healing truths of the great wisdom traditions may be expressed in clear and accessible terms.

Hampton Roads Publishing Company
. . . for the evolving human spirit

Hampton Roads Publishing Company
publishes books on a variety of subjects including
metaphysics, health, complementary medicine,
visionary fiction, and other related topics.

For a copy of our latest catalog,
call toll-free, 800-766-8009,
or send your name and address to:

Hampton Roads Publishing Company, Inc.
1125 Stoney Ridge Road
Charlottesville, VA 22902
e-mail: hrpc@hrpub.com
www.hrpub.com